A Training Effectiveness Evaluation of Leathernet

ABSTRACT

The author evaluates a Distributed Interactive Simulation (DIS) system known as LeatherNet to determine its abilities in fulfilling the long term Modeling and Simulation (M&S) goals of the United States Marine Corps. LeatherNet is a DIS compatible, virtual simulation system that is being developed to demonstrate the capabilities of today's simulation technology for military applications. The author developed an evaluation methodolgy that evaluates LeatherNet's ability to enhance traditional Marine Corps training. An evaluation was conducted by subject matter experts at the Marine Corps Ait Ground Combat Center, 29 Palms, Ca. Analysis of results show that LeatherNet is effective in enhancing traditional live fire training methods despite its limited development. The author presents lessons learned related to this type of evaluation, and provides recommendations for further research. Additionally, the author recommends actions to be taken by the Marine Corps to optimize the benefits of LeatherNet and similar simulation products.

TABLE OF CONTENTS

I. INTRODUCTION

A.   PURPOSE OF THIS THESIS

The purpose of this thesis is to assist in the evaluation of the capabilities of today's simulation technology with regard to achieving the long-term Modeling and Simulation goals of the United States Marine Corps. This thesis will develop a methodology to evaluate Distributed Interactive Simulation (DIS) systems and apply that methodology to a simulation system known as LeatherNet. Specifically, this research will evaluate user perceptions of LeatherNet's current capabilities in terms of enhancing traditional training methods.

During the last decade, computer technology has experienced an exceptional growth in capability and enabled the development of sophisticated simulators that can accurately model many aspects of the real world [Ref. 1:p. 19]. At the same time, defense appropriations have been significantly reduced, forcing the armed forces to find innovative and more efficient methods of training personnel [Ref. 2:p. 1-6]. Modeling and Simulation (M & S) systems that are currently available today demonstrate a great deal of potential in meeting the needs of tomorrow's armed forces, but much work remains to be done.

B.   SCOPE OF THIS THESIS

The scope of this thesis is limited by several factors. The Marine Corps' long term simulation goals are very broad and will require much more analysis than can be done by one person in the limited time frame of thesis research. Furthermore, LeatherNet itself is in the very early stages of development and will not be fully functional during the time when this research is accomplished. Therefore, the evaluation will be limited to Build 1, which focuses on a dismounted infantry company conducting the Range 400 exercise at Marine Corps Air Ground Combat Center (MCAGCC), 29 Palms, Ca.

C. ASSUMPTIONS

Resources in the Department of Defense (DOD) will continue to be constrained. Marine Corps missions and roles will remain relatively the same as currently defined. The Services will continue to move toward a joint forces oriented operational, training and support environment.

D. FUTURE VISION OF THE USMC

The Marine Corps has articulated its vision for the Twenty-first Century in both the Marine Corps Long Range Plan and the Marine Air Ground Task Force (MAGTF) Masterplan 1990-2000 (MMP). This vision is based upon changes in the world situation, changes in the focus of our national security strategy and estimates of the capabilities of future technology. The vision states that the Marine Corps must retain a clear aggregate usefulness--multi-purpose forces that can operate across the spectrum of conflict [Ref. 3:p. 4-1]. A solid understanding of this vision is necessary to understand the needs and requirements of tomorrow's Marine Corps.

1. National Military Strategy

a. Collapse of the Soviet Union

In response to the changing world situation, the National Security Strategy of the United States has undergone a significant change. The balance of power that was in place since the end of World War II disintegrated with the collapse of the Warsaw Pact and the world situation became increasingly more uncertain. America's National Security Strategy changed its focus from high-intensity global conflict to mid-intensity regional conflict [Ref. 3:p. 4-1]. While the chances of a high intensity nuclear war between the superpowers has decreased, the potential for numerous conflicts of varying intensity and nature has increased. [Ref. 4:p. 19]

The last five years have also seen a great deal of uncertainty develop in regions critical to our national interests; such as the Persian Gulf and the Caribbean. The U.S. found itself reacting to a wide variety of regional crises that cropped up rather rapidly and unexpectedly. These low to mid-intensity regional conflicts called for a quick

2

response by flexible forces much different than the forces prepared to defend western civilization from an all out war with the Warsaw Pact.

b.   *Increased Operational Tempo*

While the end of the Cold War decreased the chances of a global nuclear conflict, there are still many threats to our national security. In fact, the number of threats from regional conflicts seems to be increasing, and U.S. armed forces have been employed in numerous locations under widely varying mission parameters [Ref. 4:p. 6]. Many components of our armed forces are stretched to the limit from reacting to these short fused, high visibility requirements. The effect of prolonged increased operational pace is reduced readiness.

c.   *Emphasis on Joint/Combined Operations*

The increased uncertainty and lack of DOD fiscal resources have greatly increased the requirement for cooperation among the armed services. With very few exceptions, most missions will be conducted by a Joint Task Force, and will include components from all of the armed services and perhaps foreign military forces as well. [Ref. 3:p. 5-5]

2.   Effects On U. S. Marine Corps

The New National Security Strategy has profound implications for the Marine Corps [Ref. 4:p. 19]. The Marine Corps survived downsizing efforts relatively unscathed. Personnel end strength was reduced from 194,000 to 174,000 [Ref. 2:p. 1-2]. This limited reduction was based on the small relative size of the Marine Corps; and the fact that the new strategy relies heavily on the expeditionary capabilities of the Corps. [Ref. 2:p. 1-5]

a.   *Reduced DOD Spending*

In response to the end of the Cold War, the Department of Defense (DOD) has cut its forces and is now moving toward a further 25% reduction by 1997. With these cuts the defense budget is still targeted at around $250 billion in fiscal year 1997 [Ref. 5:p. 4].

3

These reductions affected the Marine Corps in several ways. In addition to personnel cuts, the Marine Corps experienced a small but significant decrease in operations and maintenance spending. The reduction in these funds by themselves is not that great but, when considered with the increased operational tempo, its effect on the Marine Corps' ability to respond quickly and decisively to the needs of the nation is significant. The Marine Corps must be able to maintain its operating forces at the highest level to meet the day to day requirements demanded by our national strategy and current funding is barely providing these resources. [Ref. 2]

The most significant trend in spending is a reduction of almost 50% in Marine Corps procurement funds over the last three years. Procurement is the hardest hit area of all USMC fiscal resources. While cutbacks in other areas are felt on a day to day basis in the operating forces, the lack of adequate procurement funds will affect the Marine Corps' ability to effectively operate throughout the next generation. The most serious ramification of this cutback is the limited ability of the Marine Corps to develop new concepts and doctrine required to meet new threats. [Ref. 2]

b.   "...From the Sea"

The Navy responded to this realignment in national strategy by shifting its focus from an open-ocean, global war to a regional, green-water outlook. This new doctrine is described in the Navy White Paper "...From the Sea" ("...FTS"). "...FTS" defines the combined vision for the Navy and Marine Corps and articulates the shape and size of the Naval Service for the next century. Marine doctrine has not been materially changed by "...FTS". However, the Navy has moved closer to a warfighting strategy that showcases the unique capabilities of the Corps. These capabilities have always been present, even if they were overlooked because of the Cold War focus on a U.S. - Soviet nuclear conflict. [Ref. 6:p. 29]

Our maritime status requires that we must defend many of our national interests at great distances from our shores. This separation from our interests is especially crucial today with the decrease of American forces based on foreign soil. Amphibious forces that are forward deployed represent a very capable and responsive force. In the cold war era Navy/Marine forces responded to numerous crises in the Dominican Republic (1965), Grenada and Lebanon (1983), Panama (1989) and the Persian Gulf (1987-1990) to include Operation Desert Storm. The new National Security Strategy has increased the requirement for Marine forces to respond quickly to a wide variety of crisis's. In the last few years, Marines have landed in Liberia, Somalia (several times), Northern Iraq, the Philippines, Bangladesh, Rwanda, Haiti and Bosnia. Many of these operations were planned and conducted in a very compressed time frame, required rapid planning and allowed for only minimal rehearsal. Currently over 18,000 Marines wait at the ready in such locations as the Arabian Sea, Mediterranean Sea, and the Western Pacific. These deployed forces represent over 30% of the USMC operating forces and 10% of all Marine forces [Ref. 7:p. 6].

c. Future Vision of USMC

The Marine Corps has elaborated on the concept of "..FTS" in its own document titled "Operational Maneuver from the Sea". Operational Maneuver from the Sea extends the concept of maneuver to naval operations. Operational Maneuver from the Sea is both a philosophy for military operations and a guide for naval force evolution [Ref.. 8:p. 1]. The goal of Operational Maneuver from the Sea is to seamlessly and continuously project combat power ashore, ensuring the rapid attainment of campaign objectives. Operations are designed to break the cohesion and integration of enemy defenses while avoiding attrition style head-on attacks. Success depends on our ability to seize fleeting opportunities and quickly take advantage of discovered enemy weaknesses. To successfully execute Operational Maneuver from the Sea on tomorrow's battlefield, we must develop new technologies and improve doctrine, organization and training so that we can execute at a faster rate and toward deeper objectives. [Ref. 8]

d. Perceived Deficiencies

The MAGTF Masterplan emphasizes numerous capabilities that are considered essential to achieving the Marine Corps' long range goal. Of particular note is the identified capability for "MAGTF Command Elements to use simulation/gaming in future operations planning to include amphibious rehearsals" [Ref. 3:p. 6-2].

5

Amphibious rehearsals present umque challenges. Many times the MAGTF receives an order that must be executed in as little as 48 hours. There is generally little opportunity to do any type of meaningful rehearsal. Rehearsal is often limited to a map exercise with limited participation of key personnel, while the unit is steaming towards the objective area. In these situations, mission success is often dependent on use of standard procedures and the initiative of small unit leaders.

In a joint or combined operation Marine landing forces will have to fight along side other forces once ashore. This presents a unique problem since there is generally no way for the commanders of the two forces to confer beforehand. The chances of a rehearsal involving both forces is even less likely.

Furthermore, the MMP goes on to identify current deficiencies that need to be overcome in order for the Marine Corps to achieve its long range vision. A recurring theme in this section is the absence of amphibious gaming facility for concept development. In this era of limited fiscal resources, concept development must be accomplished without the large research and development efforts of the past. Therefore, developing and implementing new concepts such as Operational Maneuver from the Sea will require innovative solutions that include the use of modeling and simulation. [Ref. 3]

Furthermore, the MMP identifies two trends; a reduction in spending and encroachment of training areas. To counter these trends, the Marine Corps must develop more cost effective methods of training to include simulation and instrumented ranges. [Ref. 3]

E.   MILITARY TECHNICAL REVOLUTION

The information age is creating a revolution in the way we conduct war. Its most visible effects are seen in the areas of computers, command and control, weapons and tactical information systems. The current Revolution in Military affairs is having a significant impact on military matters of all Nations, but especially on the United States [Ref. 9:p. 1]. Goure defines the Military Technical Revolution as "an order of magnitude increase in the capability to wage wars and engage in combat resulting from a new synthesis of military hardware, doctrine and operational concepts, military organization, and command, control and communications" [Ref. 10]. The Military Technology Revolution is expected to increase the relative combat effectiveness of U.S. Forces, help hedge against the rise of new threats and most significantly, help U.S. defense planners deal with the budgetary and political constraints on military policy in the years ahead [Ref. 9:p. 14].

1. Increased Capability of Computers

Almost every area of computer technology has demonstrated quantum growth in capability during the last decade. For instance the processing power of a single chip has increased by a factor of ten [Ref. 1:p. 19]. More significantly, the increase in capability has come at a greatly reduced cost. An image generator that cost $1,500,000 a decade ago now costs less than $150,000 [Ref. 1:p. 19]. Additionally, memory storage technology in the form of silicon-based Dynamic Random Access Memory chips has also shown dramatic improvement. Since their introduction, DRAM's storage capacities have been quadrupling every three years [Ref. 11: A-8].

Most industry experts expect the current trends of rapid growth of computer capabilities to continue into the next century. Additionally, their relative costs are expected to continue to decline. The military computer of the year 2001 is expected to operate at clock speeds of 2 Ghz or faster, an order of magnitude improvement over today's best rates [Ref. 12:p. 45]. The Marine Corps Modeling and Simulation Master Plan provides the following estimates: DRAMs will increase from a current capability of 16 megabits to 64 megabits in 1996 and 256 megabits in 2000. By 2010, electro-optical and optical storage technologies will be further developed, providing even greater speed and capacity. In the area of network technology, data transfer rates will increase from the current limit of 155 Mbits/sec to 2.4 Gbits/sec. By the year 2000, optical switching technologies will replace existing switches and therefore reduce a great bottleneck in networks. Computer image generation systems are expected to improve from their

7

current limits of a display rate of 1 million polygons/sec and a refresh rate of 100 million pixels/sec to 12 million polygons/sec and 3 billion pixels/sec. [Ref. 11]

2.   Distributed Interactive Simulation

One of the results of the computer age is the ability to develop systems that simulate the world in a very realistic manner. More importantly, techniques to link simulators of various types over long distances have created whole new dimensions to the use of simulators. This capability to link separate simulators together allows the simulator to be used for more than just individual or crew training. When networked, these simulators can share a common database and operate in the same virtual world. The users of the systems are able to see and interact with each other as if they were actually sharing the same battlefield. This common battlefield could then be used for combined arms training, mission rehearsal, or tactical concept development and validation. [Ref. 13:p. 15]

The use of a virtual battlefield has many advantages. There is no wear and tear on vehicles, no ammunition or fuel is expended, and units do not have to deploy to remote locations to conduct training. Furthermore, scenarios or techniques that are too dangerous to rehearse with real equipment can be done safely in the virtual world with opportunity to reenact and debrief the experience.

The concept that enables the creation of these virtual worlds 1s known as Distributed Interactive Simulation (DIS). DIS is defined as

> ...an infrastructure for linking simulations of various types at multiple locations to create realistic, complex, virtual "worlds" for the simulation of highly interactive activities. This infrastructure brings together systems built for separate purposes, technologies from different eras, products from different vendors and platforms from various services and permits them to interoperate. DIS exercises are intended to support a mixture of virtual entities (human in the loop simulators), live entities (operational platforms and test and evaluation systems), and constructive entities (wargames and automated simulations) [Ref. 14:p. 1]

8

a.   Description

DIS is both the name of a technique and a communications protocol. While it is still in the early developmental stage, it has demonstrated immense potential to fulfill many of the military's desired requirements. DIS is not a static thing, like a piece of computer hardware, but a dynamic capability that will continue to expand and incorporate new technology over time. [Ref. 15:p. 1]

In a DIS exercise each computer creates entities that are represented in the virtual world. The entities could be vehicles, aircraft, personnel or inanimate objects such as terrain features. During the course of the simulation, each entity must update all others as to its activities. Each time an entity moves or changes in some manner, it must update the rest of the virtual world DIS is more that just a virtual simulator, it is a method for creating seamless interactions between entities that that are created by simulators of different types. [Ref. 15:p. 3]

DIS is designed around several principles. By using an object/event architecture, DIS does not require information about non-changing entities to be transmitted. This design greatly reduces the amount of Protocol Data Units (PDU) that must be sent. Simulation nodes can be considered to be autonomous, therefore the transmitting node broadcasts information about itself to all others; and it is the responsibility of the receiving node to calculate whether or not it is affected by the event. Each node transmits the "absolute truth" about its activities; and receiving nodes are responsible for perceiving the information and presenting it in a realistic manner. This may require degradation of information in order to present a realistic appearance of a distant or obscured object. Dead reckoning algorithms are used to extrapolate data about nearby entities in between updates. This allows nodes to maintain simplified representations of nearby nodes and reduces the amount of information that needs to be exchanged. Current DIS performance standards are generally driven by latency constraints of 100 milliseconds. Humans cannot distinguish differences in time less than this amount; and that creates the effect of operating in real time. [Ref. 14:p. 15]

9

DIS communications architecture is based on the User Datagram Protocol. Separate nodes communicate by exchanging PDUs that are defined as part of the interface standard. PDUs may be exchanged over either local or wide area networks. Since there is no central computer, each node must broadcast information about itself to the rest of the world. In large DIS exercises the amount of traffic overwhelms even the best network interface processors. Therefore, data traffic control mechanisms such as multicast groups must be utilized. [Ref. 14:p. 16]

b. Current Capabilities

In 1992 the DIS PDU standard and communication architecture was successfully demonstrated at the Interservice/Industry Training Simulation and Education Conference. This initial demonstration allowed more than 30 simulators from more than 20 organizations to be linked together on an Ethernet LAN using DIS PDUs. The scenario included maritime, air to air, air to ground, ground to air and land operations. This demonstration proved the viability of linking heterogeneous simulators based on different technologies and built by different organizations. [Ref. 14:p. 21]

The Army's 73 Easting project demonstrated the capability to analyze an actual battle, reconstruct the salient details of the battle and then to simulate the battle in a training exercise [Ref. 15:p. 31]. Inthis project, the Army was able to recreate an actual engagement fought during Desert Storm and analyze it in a training environment.

In November, 1994, the Advanced Research Projects agency (ARPA), with the Defense Modeling and Simulation Office and the services, conducted an exercise known as Synthetic Theater of War-Europe (STOW-E) Various simulations of combat vehicles, ships and aircraft were integrated with tactical simulators and live units operating on instrumented ranges as part of the NATO Exercise Atlantic Resolve. In all, sixteen sites, generating 2100 combat platforms on two continents, were seamlessly linked together. This demonstrated the potential of this technology to reduce the costs associated with large exercises and increase the effectiveness of these exercises. [Ref. 16]

c. Current Challenges

DIS has demonstrated immense potential for revolutionizing military training, however it is not yet a mature technology and many challenges remain. One of the most important challenges is the development of a complete architecture. A comprehensive systems architecture is necessary to provide guidance to independent developers to apply standards in a consistent manner. This architecture must define major system components, the functions of each component and the interfaces required. [Ref. 14:p. 35] This development is currently being addressed by the DIS Workshop, but much work remains.

Another current challenge is achieving equality with respect to resolution. Interoperability is the heart of DIS. One of the main requirements of interoperability is the development of a common synthetic environment. Since DIS aims at connecting heterogeneous simulators, it must insure that each simulator "sees" the same image in the same way. A simulator that has higher fidelity would have an unfair advantage over other simulators that it interacts with. In particular, obtaining environmental correlation between different simulators is may be the most complex challenge facing the DIS community. [Ref. 14:p. 37]

To insure realistic representation of entities, commonly developed and accepted procedures for Verification, Validation and Accreditation must be developed. This development will require a great deal of cooperation between military, industry and research agencies. [Ref. 14:p. 39]

d. Expected Potential

ARPA estimates that DIS will eventually be able to support large scale exercises with 100,000 entities. These entities will be a mix of live, constructive and virtual simulations. These simulations will be a seamless integration of different types of simulators that are located in widely dispersed locations. ARPA plans on demonstrating this capability in an exercise called Synthetic Theater of War-97 (STOW-97). [Ref. 15:p. 42]

F.   USMC MODELING AND SIMULATION VISION

1.   Defense Modeling And Simulation Initiative (DMSI)

Recognizing the importance of modeling and simulation, and the difficulties involved with the introduction of such revolutionary technology, the DOD published the Defense Modeling and Simulation Initiative. DMSI describes an overall vision for the application of modeling and simulation throughout the Department of Defense.   [Ref. 17]

a.   Policy

The purpose of the DMSI is promote the effective and efficient use of modeling and simulation within DOD by:

- Establishing OSD cognizance and facilitating coordination among DOD modeling and simulation activities.

- Promoting the use of interoperability standards and protocols where appropriate.

- Stimulating joint use, high return modeling and simulation investments. [Ref. 17:p. 1.1]

b.   Vision

DMSI envisions a situation where modeling and simulation will allow CINCs to train and rehearse their forces in realistic scenarios despite the drawdown of forces from overseas bases. Additionally, modeling and simulation can help to ensure credibility for systems that could never be fully tested in a peacetime environment. Modeling and simulation must be able to support test and validation of new concepts, provide the means for war fighting rehearsals and preparation of forces, and allow commanders and their staffs to assess, and visualize the simulated consequences of execution of their campaign plans. Finally, like everyone else suffering through the current fiscal draught, the modeling and simulation community will have to do more with less.

2.   Marine Corps Modeling And Simulation Master Plan

Based on the guidance provided by the DMSI and its own assessment of the future, the Marine Corps established the Marine Corps Modeling and Simulation Master

Plan (MCMSMP). The previous Commandant of the Marine Corps, General Carl E. Mundy stated that "MCMSMP articulates the vision and associated end states for the Marine Corps modeling and simulation (M&S) environment. It provides a common structure for coordinating efforts within the Total Force, defines relationships between participating organizations, describes key technical issues and assesses the current state of M&S technology." [Ref. 11]

More recently, the Commandant of the Marine Corps, General Charles C. Krulak emphasized the importance of modeling and simulation in his Commandant's Planning Guidance. He states that effective training is the key to maintaining our warfighting edge in an era of scarce resources. The use of simulation can make subsequent field training more effective. Furthermore, he expects trainers to maximize the return on every dollar spent by making use of interactive training devises and simulators. [Ref. 19]

a. Policy

"The Marine Corps will acqmre and apply modeling and simulation (M&S) technologies effectively and efficiently to support Marine Corps roles and missions" [Ref. 11 :p. 1-3]. The MCMSMP sets the course for the Marine Corps use of modeling and simulation over the next several decades. Its basic assumptions are that the Marine Corps of the future will have to do more with fewer resources and more constraints, therefore it must take advantage of modeling and simulation opportunities to remain responsive to the needs of the nation. MCMSMP provides an explanation of modeling and simulation terms and concepts, and predictions of future (M&S) capabilities that are understandable to the average Marine. The document also provides guidance on management objectives, investment strategy and assigns responsibility to major commands.

b. Envisioned End States

The envisioned end state is best summarized by the following statement: "The Marine Corps will maximize warfighting capability by exploiting interoperable world class M&S" [Ref. 11:p. 1-9]. The vision aims at improving mission performance across the Total Force (including Marine Reserve units) and optimizing Marine Corps

13

participation m DOD M&S activities. The Marine Corps environment envisions augmenting rather than replacing traditional live training at all echelons. The envisioned Marine Corps end states are as follows:

- Exercise any size Total Force MAGTF as part of combined or joint operations from home bases, aboard ship, or forward deployed through the seamless integration of live, virtual and constructive simulations.

- Conduct mission planning in a distributed environment.

- Conduct mission preview and rehearsal on land or sea at all levels, from the individual Marine to MEF within 48 hours of notification.

- Validate Marine Corps requirements and doctrine using Modeling & Simulation as a primary tool.

- Participate in the fundamental improvement of the acquisition process by simulation before "we buy, build or fight."

- Merge Modeling & Simulation and C3 systems.

- Support every major weapon system in the Marine Corps with a simulator that can be networked into a common synthetic environment.

- Use Modeling & Simulation as a primary decision support tool. [Ref. 11:p. 1-12]

G. EVOLUTIONARY ACQUISITION

1. Background

Many of the large DOD computer systems acquired in the past were the product of the "grand design" methodology. This methodology attempts to design and field a system with all functionality and user requirements implemented at one time. Over the past several decades many individuals in government and industry have been dissatisfied with the "grand design" methodology of acquiring technology, particularly the technology involved in command and control systems. Perceived problems included the excessive time required to develop and field the system, failure to meet users needs and reliance on obsolete technology. A study conducted by the Armed Forces Communications and Electronic Association (AFCEA) at the request of the Assistant

Secretary of Defense for C^3I systems concluded that evolutionary acquisition is the best approach for fielding successful C3I systems that keep pace with technology, user requirements and expectations. The DOD defines evolutionary acquisition as: "...an approach in which a core capability is fielded, and the system design has a modular structure and provisions for future upgrades and changes as requirements are refined". Furthermore, evolutionary acquisition is the preferred approach for the procurement of complex, software-intensive C^3I systems. [Ref. 20]

The study recommended that program specifications should specify an integration architecture that would accommodate evolving requirements as well as system growth in functions and performance, robust software migration and open interfaces with other systems. Furthermore, the study recommends that specifications should define a core system for initial fielding and should outline subsequent upgrades in terms of objective requirements. Each upgrade would be defined in greater detail prior to implementation. Lastly, users should participate throughout the system's evolution to provide meaningful and timely feedback. [Ref. 20:p. VIII]

2.   Applicability

The official DOD definition of a command, control and communication system is:

> The facilities, equipment, communications, procedures, and
> personnel essential to a commander for planning, directing,
> and controlling operations of assigned forces pursuant to
> the missions assigned.

This definition can be expanded to include models and simulations used for mission preview and rehearsal. Considering the complex nature of DIS systems, the current pace of changing technology and the potential for changing user requirements, an evolutionary approach is the most preferred. [Ref. 20]

H.   SUMMARY

This chapter illustrates that the Marine Corps faces many challenges as it moves into the next century. Reductions in spending, encroachment of training areas and the rapidly changing requirements of the National Security Strategy represent major obstacles to meeting these challenges. Successful development of new concepts such as Operational Maneuver from the Sea will require better and more innovative solutions.

Additionally, Marine forces must overcome many challenges related to maintaining a capable, flexible, forward deployed force in readiness. The capabilities to conduct mission rehearsal and training of forces embarked aboard amphibious shipping are especially critical.

Recent improvements in simulation technology represent immense potential for military applications and can contribute to overcoming many challenges that currently exist. The Marine Corps has stated its commitment to make effective use of this technology to enhance its training effectiveness and ability to respond to future developments.

Development of these applications will be a lengthy process and ongoing process; systems must be flexible to meet the evolving needs of users. Therefore, an evolutionary acquisition strategy must be used to support new requirements and take advantage of new developments.

This research will use a case study of LeatherNet to evaluate the ability of today's simulation technology to meet the future needs of the Marine Corps.

I.   OUTLINE OF CHAPTERS

1.   Chapter II. Simulation Systems

In this chapter, the benefits and limitations of simulators are discussed. Considerations for evaluating the effectiveness of training alternatives are presented. The chapter discusses the background and evaluation methodologies of SIMNET and TTES. The chapter concludes with background information on LeatherNet.

2.   Chapter III. Methodology

In this chapter, the methodology of the evaluation is presented. The driving factors behind the design of the methodology are discussed. Additionally, a step by step process is outlined to provide details into how, where and when certain tasks were accomplished.

3.   **Chapter IV. Analysis of Data**

In this chapter, the data that was collected during the evaluation is analyzed. Data is presented in graphical format along with a discussion of that data. Additionally, evaluator comments are analyzed where appropriate.

4.   **Chapter V. Summary and Recommendations**

This chapter summarizes the issues, their significance to the Marine Corps and suggestions to optimize the use of LeatherNet and similar systems. Also presented are lessons learned about this type of evaluation and recommendations for future research.

II. SIMULATION SYSTEMS

A. BACKGROUND

The military has had a long history of using simulation in training for combat. Like many other inherently dangerous activities, combat must be simulated in order to train personnel in a safe environment. The Chairman of DOD's Simulation Policy Study, General Paul Gorman, testifying to the Congress in 1992 stated that "All tactical training short of combat is a simulation" [Ref. 21:p. 4].

DOD Directive 5000.59 defines simulation as "...a method for implementing a model over time, or a technique for testing, analysis or training in which real world systems are used, or where real-world and conceptual systems are reproduced by a model". The directive further defines a model as "...a physical, mathematical, or otherwise logical representation of a system, entity, phenomenon or process" [Ref. 21:p. 3].

Simulators can be classified as one of three types; live, constructive or virtual. A live simulation is any simulation in which personnel operate actual military equipment, such as a field firing exercises or tactical maneuvers. A Constructive simulation is a computer driven war game which combines simulated forces with simulated systems. A virtual simulation provides a view of the world to the user and allows an interaction with objects in the virtual world. Virtual simulations usually emphasize real time, human decision making. [Ref. 22]

B. BENEFITS OF SIMULATORS

Simulation provides numerous benefits to military forces. At a simulation industry conference in November, 1994, Army Chief of Staff, General Gordon Sullivan stated: "Simulators allow users to experience new realities, keep the intellectual juices flowing and most importantly, reduce resistance to change" [Ref. 1]. In this era of rapid change for our military forces, these traits are extremely valuable.

Simulators can be used to reduce the cost of training or to increase the amount of training for a given cost. For instance, a TOW practice missile costs about $9,000; a single shot in the Precision Gunnery Training System costs about $.05. Furthermore, use of the simulator reduces the wear and tear on the system itself and reduces the need to train at a remote location.   [Ref. 23:p. 18]

Simulators allow the operator to train for dangerous conditions in a safe environment. Many aviation simulators can create emergency scenarios that would be too dangerous to actually perform in a real aircraft. More importantly, simulation of combat operations allow commanders to take risks that are not acceptable in other types of training. This risk taking includes taking casualties and material losses.

In many cases, simulators can provide more accurate performance measures than the actual equipment. The Indoor Simulated Marksmanship Trainer inserts laser electronics into a modified weapon and shoots against realistic video images projected on laser sensitive screen. This simulator provides the trainer with detailed, accurate measures of performance for each shot. It allows for problem diagnosis, prescriptive drills and immediate feedback. This kind of measurement is far more informative than what could be accomplished on the firing range. [Ref. 23:p. 19]

Simulators help us to understand not only what happened during an actual exercise, but more importantly, why things happened. Simulators do not fully replicate the real world but only model a simplified version of the real world. This simplified version is what enables users to better understand the real world. [Ref. 24]

C.   LIMITATIONS OF SIMULATORS

The DOD reports that simulators also have some limitations which inhibit their use. For example, simulators have a limited capability to represent the complex conditions involved in such activities as tactical aviation. Simulators can also cause a disorientation known as "simulator sickness" if visual and motion cues are not carefully synchronized.   [Ref. 25]

Orlansky also states that simulators may instill incorrect habits, or cause inadequate or misleading training if the fidelity of visual representation is not correct. A solid understanding of a simulator's limitations is vital to effectively using it in a training scenario. [Ref. 26]

D. EFFECTIVENESS OF TRAINING

The Marine Corps believes that realistic, standards-based, performance oriented training is the key to combat effectiveness. Training for combat is a difficult endeavor, and no training method will fully replicate the stress and rigors of actual combat. The Marine Corps envisions simulation use to enhance or augment rather than replace traditional training methods. [Ref. 23]

Orlansky defines effectiveness in a training system as the measure of the extent to which one method of training succeeds in helping trainees acquire the skills and knowledge specified. In terms of a simulator, this translates to how well a system increases a trainee's knowledge or skill on real world equipment. [Ref. 26]

The Rand corporation reports that the effectiveness of a simulator cannot be judged for all uses by a single test, but must be determined for each distinct use. To assess the effectiveness of a simulator, one must assess the effect of the experience on the participants rather than the degree of realism produced by the simulator. This trait is referred to as transferability. If the task performed has strong transferability (such as driving a tank) then performance on a simulator can be compared to definite standards as well as performance on the actual equipment. Tasks with weak transferabilities (such as with larger unit battle-oriented proficiencies) cannot be reduced to a set of definite standards and are more difficult to compare to real world performance. In this case, the effectiveness of the simulator must be subjectively judged by subject matter experts. [Ref. 27]

E. COST EFFECTIVENESS OF TRAINING

Development of a new system generally implies the expectation of an additional or enhanced capability be acquired in return for the investment. Determining the cost-effectiveness of simulation systems has traditionally focused heavily on the cost and not on the training value. This frequently leads to cheap solutions which do not fully support the user. [Ref. 28]

In this era of declining budgets, expensive training systems need to be justified with validated data for both cost and effectiveness in preparing for operational readiness. The Office of the Assistant Secretary of Defense for Force Management and Personnel has a requirement to monitor the effectiveness of training within DOD to ensure that resources are properly allocated. However, this endeavor is complicated in that practices for determining Cost and Training effectiveness are not standard across the services. The Institute for Simulation and training points out that cost/effectiveness analysis should focus on:

- Whether the device training can save some portion of the more costly field training.

- Whether device training can enable subsequent on-weapon training to start and finish at a higher level of performance, thereby increasing the return-on-investment from weapons training.

- Whether the benefit of device training exceeds other lower cost training such as classroom instruction, map or terrain-board exercises. [Ref. 28]

The Program Manager for the Army's Simulation, Training, & Instrumentation Command (STRICOM) stated that the military has generally been unable to conduct hard analysis of training alternatives because we have not properly measured the results of training: yet despite the cost of training systems, no comprehensive assessment program is in place [Ref. 28]. Cost training effectiveness analysis generally attempt to convert the benefits of a system into some metric which can be compared to cost, this usually requires some very subjective judgments [Ref. 29]. Orlansky points out that there is a notable absence of reported data on the costs of collective training, especially in operational units [Ref. 26].

A study conducted by the Defense Manpower Data Center (DMDC) illustrated some of the difficulty in assessing the value of particular training methods. The study stated that DOD had standard and reliable methods of cost comparison, but there is no such method available for the comparison of the effectiveness of alternative systems. The study states that military value can only be reflected in the degree of combat success; and this value can only be empirically assessed in combat which is impractical. [Ref. 31]

EFFECTIVENESS

		LESS	SAME	MORE
	LESS	?	+	+
COST	SAME	-	?	+
	MORE	-	-	?

Table 1. Orlansky's Decision Model [Ref. 26]

Simulators in the military have generally been sought to provide equal effectiveness at a lower cost than actual equipment, but Orlansky states that the military should seek simulators that provide increased effectiveness at the same or lower costs. Table 1 illustrates Orlansky's model, where (-) represents rejection, (?) represents uncertainty and (+) represents adoption. Using Orlansky's model as a guide, the military should strive to procure simulators that provide the same or greater effectiveness at the same or lesser costs. The focus on developing simulators that provide increased effectiveness has generally been neglected in the military. This condition stems from the fact that assessing the effectiveness of large forces in simulated combat is a difficult and not well developed art. [Ref. 25]

Figure 1 illustrates the spectrum of realism in training and the relative costs associated with each type of scenario. Actual combat is obviously the most realistic, however it also presents the maximum cost and risk.

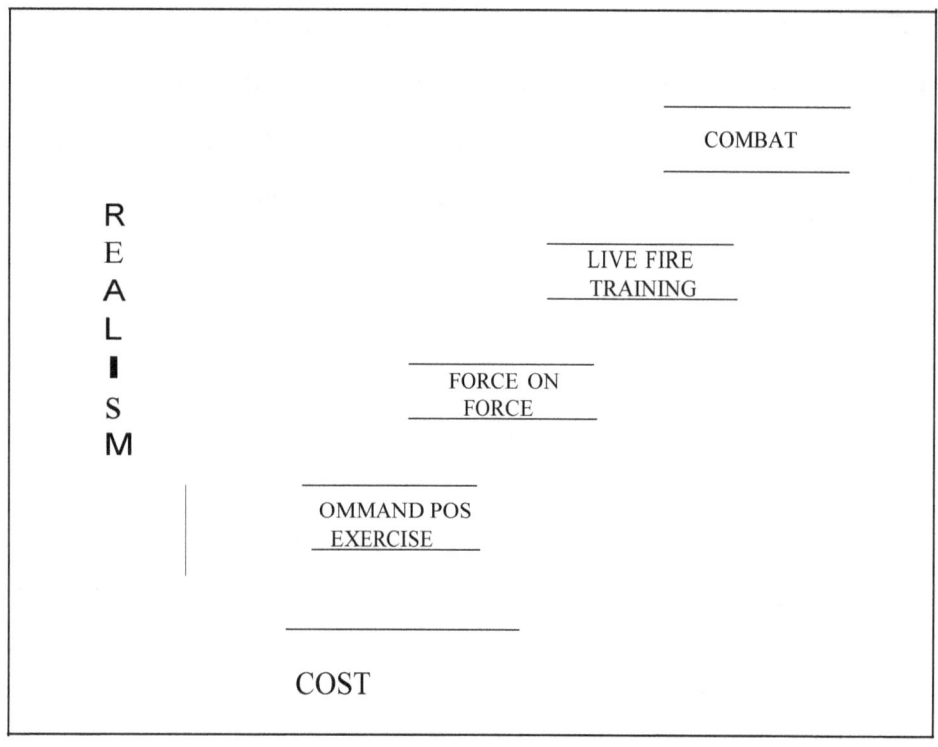

Figure 1. Realism Versus Cost

Live fire training represents the closest replication to actual combat. Live fire exercises allow the user to actually fire their weapons, preferably with quantitative and qualitative feedback on performance. Live fire training is limited in its ability to portray enemy forces, limited by safety constraints, and is expensive in terms of equipment and material.

Force-on-force training allows a unit to operate against an actual enemy. Weapons are employed and may use blank ammunition and performance feedback devises such as Multiple Integrated Laser Engagement System (MILES). Force on force training is limited by its ability to effectively exercise large forces and its ability to provide objective feedback. Force-on-force exercise are expensive, time consuming and provide diminishing return to the small unit as the size of the exercise increases.

Command post exercises are conducted by commanders and staffs using maps and communications equipment only. They provide the unit the opportunity to exercise its command and control functions, but are limited in their ability to accurately portray forces engaged in combat.

Figure 2 illustrates the relationship between effectiveness and the relative cost of different types of training tools. The ability of computers to quickly process large amounts of information and present it in a useable format make for very effective training devices. The relative cost of computer simulations exceed the other types, but that relative cost is quickly declining with advances in technology. Manual wargames made up a significant majority of simulations before the introduction of computers. Map exercises are still used by many commanders and their staffs to train their subordinates. This is especially the case when units are deployed to areas away from supporting establishments.

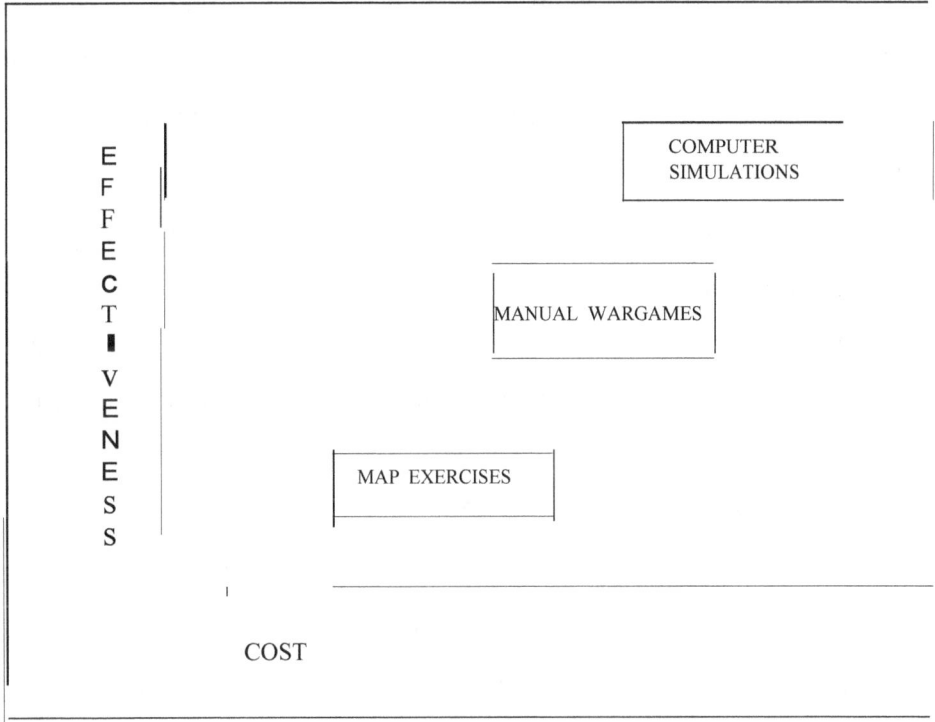

Figure 2. Effectiveness Versus Cost

Comparing Figures 1 and 2 shows that the optimal training scenario combines the realism of combat with the information processing capability of computers. However, training cannot rely solely on one method to achieve effectiveness. The optimum

25

combination of the use of simulators and actual equipment must be determined in order to take advantage of that technology.   [Ref. 26]

Analysis of the simulator's effectiveness must first consider the effectiveness and limitations of the traditional training methods. Once these traits are established, a training plan must be developed to enhance the effectiveness of the traditional training methods. In this context, the training effectiveness of a simulator can then be established.

F.   EVALUATIONS OF OTHER SIMULATORS

1.   SIMNET

a. Background

SIMNET was developed by the Advanced Projects Research Agency (ARPA) as a test-bed for linking large numbers of combat simulators within a single site and across geographically separated sites. ARPA has transitioned SIMNET to the Army at several sites. The system is continually evolving, and specific capabilities may vary from site to site [Ref. 32:p. 3].

SIMNET uses computer-generated imagery to create a simulated battleground over which units may move, shoot and communicate. Various weapon systems and terrain features appear and behave much as they would in a field setting. Weapon systems can see each other and kill each other with realistic probabilities [Ref. 32:p. 3].

The primary components of SIMNET are manned combat vehicle simulators representing the Ml Abrams tank and the M2 Bradley fighting vehicle. Each simulator module includes space for all crew members, and each crew member has a vision block providing views of the computer-generated battlefield. Simulators are equipped with the controls for selected weapon systems which can be used against other entities, armor protection and communication systems. Their movement is influenced by terrain and they are subject to fuel and ammunition constraints. [Ref. 32]

The simulator provides its crew members with the illusion of operating a real vehicle over real terrain. The crew operates with many of the capabilities and constraints experienced in the real world. Many of the SIMNET facilities include simulated tactical operations centers and simulated command posts which appear on the battlefield but cannot view it. [Ref. 32]

A plan view display and stealth vehicle are available to support observation of SIMNET exercises. The plan view display provides a graphic view of portions of the battleground, with icons representing entities. The stealth vehicle is an invisible vehicle that provides a view of the battlefield which can late be played back to support a debrief. [Ref. 32:p. 4]

b. Evaluation Methodology

SIMNET has been the subject of numerous evaluations and studies. The Army and other DOD agencies continue to analyze its capabilities. However, a complete determination of its capabilities is limited by scarce resources. [Ref. 32:p. 5]

Instructors at the U.S. Army Armor school assessed the capabilities of SIMNET to support institutional training. Small groups of instructors reviewed the tasks taught in various courses and rated the degree to which they could be trained using simulation. Personnel in operational units have also assessed the system's training capabilities, but this effort did not provide a detailed analysis of which tasks could be trained with SIMNET. The Army Research Institute analyzed armor operations to identify activities performed in combat and attempted to perform a sample of these tasks on SIMNET. This resulted in a very detailed analysis of SIMNET's capabilities, but it addressed only platoon level operations. [Ref. 32:p. 5]

A study conducted by the Army Armor and Engineer Board found that soldiers using SIMNET improved their performance as much if not better than soldiers performing the same tasks in actual equipment. While the test could not produce significant statistical data, test participants felt that SIMNET was useful at training troop leading procedures, command and control, land navigation and teamwork. They cited the ability to place platoons in a stressful situation and keep pressure on the platoons throughout the exercise as one of the system's best features. [Ref. 33]

The U.S. Air Force Tactical Air Command conducted a study of SIMNET to evaluate its potential for training pilots in the close air support environment. The test participants felt that the simulation eliminated the normally controlled training environment and that they were involved in a competition against an adversary. However, SIMNET did not provide an adequate level of realism for the aircrew needs. Specific requested enhancements included: increased field of view, improved aircraft flight fidelity, improved terrain features and improved visual target acquisition capability. [Ref. 33]

2. TTES

a. Background

The Team Tactical Engagement Simulator (TTES) is part of service-wide effort to apply modeling and simulation techniques to individual combatants in the infantry, law enforcement, security and special operations forces. The TTES Advanced Technology demonstration effort began in 1993 and will continue through 1996. The envisioned system will be fielded between 2002 and 2006. TTES emphasizes tactical decision-making in a dynamic synthetic environment (DSE) which will complement live fire field training. The DSE includes a dynamic representation of the physical environment and a behavioral representations of friendlies, hostiles and neutrals. One of the most valuable assets of TTES is that its designed to teach "when" to shoot as well as "how" to shoot. [Ref. 34]

The envisioned TTES system will fully immerse fire team members in a common virtual reality using helmet mounted displays with audio capabilities. Multiple trainees will be able to interact with each other and computer generated entities via a radio frequency using DIS protocols. [Ref. 34]

b. Evaluation Methodology

An evaluation of TTES was conducted in conjunction with a Marine Corps training exercise and system demonstration. The participants in the evaluation included twenty-one subject matter experts from various military and civilian law enforcement agencies. The participants received some familiarization with TTES and then participated in a hostage rescue exercise in a MOUT building that had been emulated on TTES. The live exercise gave participants the opportunity to compare the actual with the virtual experience. Participants then conducted the same exercise on a one-man TTES that was set up on site. The subject group was given questionnaires to evaluate the importance of various factors making up the simulation capabilities that might be included in TIES simulations. Respondents were also asked to rate the perceived TTES capability to emulate these factors, both in the system's present form and as TTES is envisioned to be fielded in the future. [Ref. 34]

The evaluation revealed that the current version of TTES is only marginally capable of providing needed training in discretionary decisions and marksmanship. The evaluators gave ratings of less than 50% to all of the fifteen categories and the average rating was only 41.8%. The major categories were ranked as follows: Marksmanship Events, Training Situations and Discretionary Decisions. However, the same study revealed that TIES demonstrates immense potential to provide the needed training. In terms of potential, the categories were ranked as follows: Discretionary Decisions, Marksmanship Events, and Training Situations. Given this data, it appears that more emphasis should be given to Discretionary Decisions. [Ref. 34]

G.   LEATHERNET

LeatherNet is a DIS compatible, virtual simulation system that is funded by the Advanced Research Projects Agency (ARPA) and is currently being developed at Marine Corps Air Ground Combat Center (MCAGCC), 29 Palms CA. This project supports the long term research being conducted by ARPA for the Synthetic Theater of War 1997 (STOW 97). [Ref. 35]

1.   STOW 97

The vision of STOW 97 is to provide a computer-based environment in which interactive human users above a certain level of Command and Control can conduct, in virtual reality, realistic wartime scenarios involving both friendly and enemy forces, observe the development of a scenario, log the major actions, review and debrief the development, and ask and playout "what if' questions. STOW 97 will be a proof of principal demonstration of large scale joint exercise conducted by live, virtual and constructive forces, connected over the Defense Simulation Internet (DSI). The number of entities (weapons, platforms squads etc.) involved will be on the order of 100,000. [Ref.35]

2. Semi-Automated Forces

Large scale DIS based simulations require the development of credible, multi-echeloned automated forces that behave in ways that accurately represent the tactical organizations that they represent. These intelligent computer generated forces will enable large free-play exercises, while requiring only a few live commanders and staff personnel. [Ref. 34] Semi-Automated Forces (SAF) provide a computer generated version of manned simulators for DIS. The purposes of SAF are cost reduction, the ability to encode human expertise and to provide a quantifiable, repeatable training environment. [Ref. 22]

3. Human Computer Interface

An interface known as CommandVu is being developed. CommandVu provides a realistic three-dimensional view of the virtual battlefield that supports multiple functions. This visualization is provided by NPSNET IV.8 and provides animation for basic behavior of MC SAF, environmental and weapons effects. It will eventually include such features as speech and gesture recognition. [Ref. 35]

4. Current Status

LeatherNet is currently being developed incrementally at 29 Palms according to the following schedule:

- Build 1

  A terrain walk of Range 400 (Dismounted Daylight Infantry Company Attack). A capability for a Company Command Element and Platoon Leaders to conduct Range 400 mission planning, briefing, rehearsal and debrief.

- Build 2

  A capability for a Company Command Element and Platoon Leaders to conduct Delta Corridor mission planning, briefing rehearsal and debrief.

- Build 3

  A capability for a Battalion Landing Team Command Element and Company Command Elements to conduct Delta Corridor mission planning, briefing rehearsal and debrief.

- Build 4

  A capability for a Regimental Landing Team Command Element and Battalion Landing Team elements to conduct Delta Corridor mission planning, briefing rehearsal and debrief.

Builds 1-2 will be completed during FY 94-95 and Builds 3-4 will be completed in FY 95 through 97. In the course of the above builds, the project will support exercises by participating Marine units. [Ref. 35]

5. USMC Vision

The Marine Corps vision of LeatherNet is to:

- Develop the USMC Semi-Automated Forces (MC SAF) capability, for implementation in STOW 97.

- Provide MCAGCC with a useful appealing training tool for mission planning, briefing, rehearsal and debriefing.

- Utilize the principle of selective fidelity to represent less critical or non-fighting elements such as sensors, communication, and other support services, which are realistically relevant combat support systems or C2 nodes but do not necessarily need modeling at the element level of detail.

- Create, in software, a realistic representation of Marine Corps command nodes both afloat and ashore, and provide the mechanism necessary which will portray the influence of one command level on the actions of subordinate levels.

- Develop, in concert with the other component services SAF, a robust technical software architecture which is sufficiently expandable to account for the unique features of USMC systems. [Ref. 35]

For the realization of the above vision, USMC SAF will create, in DIS, a representation of the attributes of a Forward presence (amphibious domain) and ground maneuver (ground domain) represented by a Marine Expeditionary Force (MEF). Models developed by the other services will used whenever appropriate. [Ref. 35]

31

The Marine Corps expects to use LeatherNet primarily to train platoon and higher level commanders in warfighting skills. These skills are collective in nature and present varying degrees of transferability. Many of these tasks can only be evaluated in a subjective manner. The anticipated payoffs for this project will include lower cost and more effective training for Marine Corps personnel and the capability to study sets of tactical alternatives. [Ref. 35]

6.   Limitations

LeatherNet is designed primarily to demonstrate the capabilities of simulation technology and is not designed to fulfill specific Marine Corps needs. While the Marine Corps will certainly benefit from the development of this project, there may be significant differences between LeatherNet and any system procured and fielded for Marine Corps units. LeatherNet is currently in the early stages of development and a detailed analysis of its capabilities and limitations is not appropriate at this time.

H.   SUMMARY

Computer simulations have a great deal of value to military forces. STOW 97 and LeatherNet represent the cutting edge of today's virtual simulation technology. To fully benefit from this technology, the Marine Corps must be an active participant in the development of this system.

Many simulation systems are designed and evaluated with the goal of cost avoidance in mind. While that is a noble goal, it does not serve the military user very well. The focus on developing simulators that provide increased effectiveness has generally been neglected in the military. Furthermore, there are no standard DOD guidelines for assessing the effectiveness of training alternatives. Evaluations of SIMNET and TTES illustrate some of the challenges of determining the effectiveness of a training system.

Evaluation of a simulator's effectiveness must be accomplished for each particular purpose. Evaluation of a simulator's effectiveness should first assess the effectiveness of the traditional training method. The simulator should then be evaluated in the context of increasing the training effectiveness of that traditional training method. From this evaluation, a plan is developed to determine the optimum combination of simulator training and traditional training.

III. METHODOLOGY

A. BACKGROUND

1. Purpose

The purpose of this research is to evaluate LeatherNet's perceived ability to fulfill the Marine Corps' long range modeling and simulation goals. This will be accomplished by focusing on LeatherNet's capabilities to enhance the perceived effectiveness of Marine Corps live fire training.

2. Assumptions

This methodology could be used with a larger group of participants and in a more robust evaluation of this type of system. However, adjustments in methodology may be required to accommodate larger and more detailed evaluations.

3. Limitations

This research was limited by several factors. The time and resources available were not sufficient to conduct an in depth analysis of the system. The number of participants was also limited by the size of the temporary LeatherNet facility and the heavy operational tempo of the units at MCAGCC. Additionally, it was not practical to conduct empirical testing of a system that is not yet fully developed.

4. Rationale

The design of this evaluation is driven by many factors, the limitations mentioned above are obviously included. The role that LeatherNet may play in Marine Corps training has also been considered. LeatherNet is located at MCAGCC, which is the Marine Corps' premier combined arms training facility, because of safety and environmental constraints at other Marine Corps bases. Active and reserve forces participate in regularly scheduled Combined Arms Exercises (CAX). The training environment at MCAGCC provides the closest replication to actual combat that today's technology will allow. The primary focus of training at MCAGCC is the integration of combined arms. This is a difficult, expensive and sometimes dangerous training goal, however, it is vital to the development of combat-effective Marine Corps units. Due to its relative importance in the training spectrum, combined arms training should be made as effective and efficient as possible. Simulation presents great potential for enhancing combined arms training, but the specific benefits of this technology have yet to be evaluated.

As Orlansky [Ref. 25] and Simpson [Ref. 30] point out, evaluating the effectiveness of training alternatives is not guided by any specific guidelines and procedures vary from service to service. Furthermore, many of the skills required for effective integration of combined arms are not easily measured in quantifiable terms. This makes it difficult to assess and compare the effectiveness of training alternatives. Gathering empirical data on these type of skills would be a long, labor intensive and expensive task. Therefore, this research will focus on the perceptions of subject matter experts to determine the training effectiveness of LeatherNet.

5.   Test **Environment**

   a.   *Selection of Functions to be evaluated*

LeatherNet is currently in the early stages of development. The current version, Build 1 is designed to provide the following capabilities:

- A terrain walk of Range 400.

- A capability for a Company Command Element to conduct R400 mission planning, briefing, rehearsal and debrief.

This research will focus on evaluating Build 1 by comparing the benefits and limitations of the traditional Range 400 exercise with those of the simulation. Range 400 is a live fire range equipped with fortified enemy positions that include simulated vehicles and obstacles. Trench lines and bunkers have been constructed in accordance with Warsaw Pact doctrine. Marine infantry companies participating in CAX's conduct Range 400 exercises to develop and refine the skills required in a daylight dismounted attack against a Soviet strongpoint. Success depends heavily on the ability of the company and platoon commanders to effectively integrate direct and indirect fire in support of maneuver.   It is a very challenging evolution for all participants, but especially for the company and platoon commanders. This research will therefore focus on evaluating the benefits of this technology for those specific billets.

b.   *Participating Personnel*

The participants in the evaluation were subject matter experts from the MCAGCC. All personnel were either infantry company or platoon commanders from the 7th Marine Regiment. All were permanently stationed at MCAGCC and had participated in at least one live fire exercise on Range 400. None of the participants were familiar with the system prior to the evaluation. None of the participants had served in combat.

c.   *Conditions of the Test*

The author arrived at MCAGCC on Tuesday, 8 August and received an orientation by the system engineer, Mr. Mack Brewer of the Mitre Corporation. Wednesday, 9 August was used for further familiarization with the system and setting up a demonstration. The evaluation was conducted on Thursday, 10 August between 9 and 12 a.m.

The test was conducted in the LeatherNet Project Facility at MCAGCC. The participants were given a brief description of the research, the background on LeatherNet and instructions on completing the questionnaires. Participants were seated in an area where they could observe the actions of the simulation and fill out their evaluations. The author was in the room for the entire time and was available for questions from participants. Mr. Brewer operated the system during the demonstration and was also available for questions.

d.   *Measures*

Participants were given questionnaires to indicate their opinion as to the effectiveness of the traditional training method and the simulator. The questionnaires were constructed with a five point Likert scale.

B.   EVALUATION PROCEDURES

    1.   Identify Perceived Benefits and Limitations of USMC Live Fire
          Training by Case Study of Range 400

A questionnaire was developed to gather subject matter expert's opinion on the effectiveness of Range 400 in providing specific training benefits for company and platoon commanders. The questionnaire was pre-tested by Naval Postgraduate School students who had participated in Range 400 exercises. The pre-testing helped to clarify the instructions and improve the format. The Range 400 Assessment questionnaire is found in Appendix A. The results of the NPS questionnaire are in Appendix B.

The questionnaire titled "Range 400 Assessment" (Appendix A) was given to the subject matter experts at MCAGCC prior to the LeatherNet demonstration. The subject matter experts were given as much time as necessary to complete the questionnaire, all finished within twenty minutes. The results of the Range 400 Assessment are provided in Appendix C.

    2.   Determine Which Benefits of R400 Can Be Provided by LeatherNet

The subject matter experts then viewed a demonstration of LeatherNet which illustrated selected capabilities of MCSAF, CommandVu and Language Enabled SAF (LE SAF). The demonstration presented a scenario with an enemy fire team occupying a defensive position. A USMC squad with machine gun and mortar support conducted an attack. The demonstration also included a brief display of armor operations. The site manager and the author narrated the demonstration and participants were able to ask questions.

Participants were then given the questionnaire titled "LeatherNet Assessment" (Appendix D) and asked to state their opinion on LeatherNet's ability to provide the same benefits as Range 400. This information was gathered in questions 4-11. The participants then ranked the traits desired in a simulator of this type according to their relative importance (Question 12, A-H).

3. Determine LeatberNet's Perceived Ability to Enhance Range 400 Exercises

Questions 13-20 of Appendix D gathered experts opinion on the ability of LeatherNet to enhance the effectiveness of the traditional training method. Question 21 then asked the experts to rank the capabilities of LeatherNet according to their relative effectiveness in overcoming the limitations of the traditional methods of training. The results of LeatherNet Assessment can be found in Appendix E.

4. Determine LeatherNet's Perceived Ability to Fulfill Modeling and Simulation End States

Questions 22-27 of Appendix D solicited the subject matter expert's opinion of LeatherNet's ability to fulfill the Marine Corps' desired M&S end states. The subject matter experts were given a brief overview of the Marine Corps' M&S vision prior to this segment.

5. Gather Subjective Data on Users Opinion of Most and Least Impressive Aspects of LeatherNet

Subject matter experts were then given an opportunity to state their opinion on what impressed them the most and least about LeatherNet. These comments are summarized in Chapter IV.

6. Gather User's Opinion on the Type of Quantitative Feedback Desired From a Simulation of This Type

Subject matter experts were then asked to provide input concerning what type of quantitative feedback they would find useful in this type of simulator. These items are discussed in Chapter IV.

C. DATA DESCRIPTION

The data collected in this evaluation was ordinal data. Participants stated their opinion on the effectiveness of the training alternatives and in some questions ranked the traits of the training alternatives. Participants stated their opinion on a five point scale indicating the degree to which they agreed with the statement in question. Participants were also asked to provide some additional feedback such as likes and dislikes concerning the simulator.

### 1.	Example of Raw Data

Table 2 presents an example of the raw data. The names of the evaluators have been removed prior to the tabulation of this data.

QUESTION	MARINE #1	MARINE #2	MARINE #3	MARINE #4	MARINE #5
4	5	4	4	4	4
5	5	5	4	4	5
6	5	5	4	5	3

Table 2. Raw Data Example

### 2.	Data Coding Schemes

Data was collected and input into tables as shown in Table 2. Each question had its own row and each Marine participating had his own column. Each cell in the table indicates a response from a particular participant to a particular question.

## D.	ANALYSIS

### 1.	Analysis Plan

The data collected in this evaluation is strictly ordinal data. All questions are either preference rankings or opinion scales. Because numbers in these types of scales have only a rank meaning, the measure of central tendency is the median. Therefore, analysis of this data will be based on the median values to determine significance. In some cases data will be plotted in a two dimensional display where effectiveness is plotted verses importance. This does not imply that the scales are anything other than ordinal data and no other manipulation was done.

### 2.	Additional Assumptions

The number of participants was very small and from a fairly homogeneous population. The average experience of the participants was very similar and somewhat limited. These factors could have unknown effects on the outcome of the evaluation.

IV.   ANALYSIS OF DATA

A.   RANGE 400

1.   Assess R400's Perceived Benefits

The perceived benefits of Range 400 exercises were examined from both a group of subject matter experts both at Naval Postgraduate School and MCAGCC. The group at NPS consisted of 11 officers who had completed a total of 71 Range 400 exercises. Five officers had served in combat, the median time in service was 12 years. The NPS group was used to pretest the questionnaire. The group at MCAGCC consisted of 5 subject matter experts with 54 total Range 400 exercises. However, it should be noted that two of the participants accounted for 42 of the total exercises. The median time in service was 3 years and none of the participants had served in combat.

Chart 1 displays the median opinion of the MCAGCC participants regarding the benefits of Range 400. The values in Chart 1 represent the median values of the participant's opinions. The numbers on the left side of the chart correspond to Questions 4-11 in Appendix A. The data for Chart 1 can be found in Appendix C.

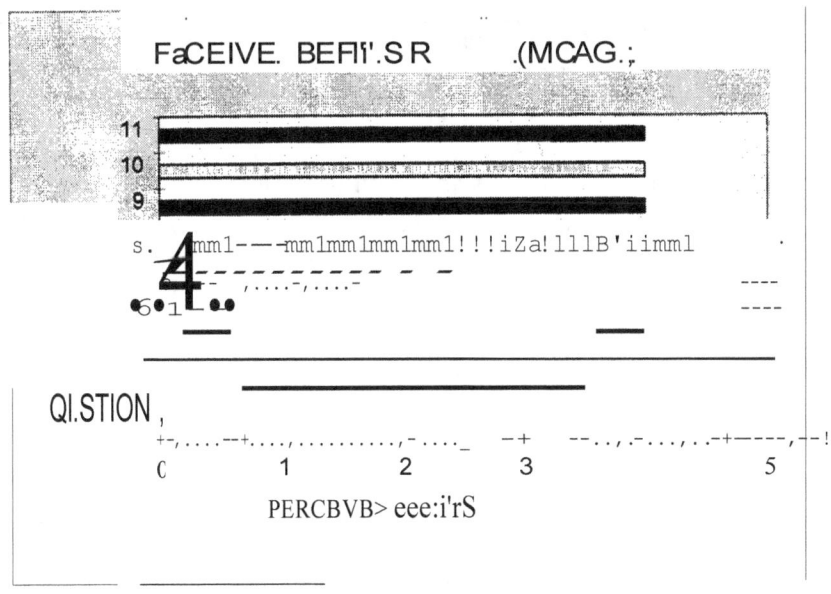

Chart 1. Perceived Benefits of Range 400

The MCAGCC participants agreed that all the listed benefits were provided by Range 400. The strongest opinions (a value of 5 in Chart 1) were stated in the following areas: (Question 5), the opportunity to conduct live fire combined arms exercise, (Question 6), the opportunity to exercise maneuver skills, (Question 7), the opportunity to exercise fire support skills, and (Question 8), the opportunity to integrate maneuver and fire support.

2.   **Rank Benefits of USMC Live Fire Training**

Table 3 illustrates the relative importance of the various benefits that may be provided from live fire exercises. The scores were compiled by taking the median value of all of the rankings (Question 12, Appendix A) and then sorting them from lowest (most important) to highest (least important). Ties were broken where possible by looking at the mean ranking for that question. The creation of a stressful environment that realistically simulates combat is the most important benefit, with tactical desionmaking in a real time environment second.

TRAIT	RANK
Stressful environment that realistically simulates combat.	1
An opportunity to exercise tactical decisionmaking skills in a real time scenario.	2
The opportunity to conduct maneuver with live fire assets.	3
The opportunity to develop maneuver skills	4
The opportunity to work with combined arms assets on one range	5
The opportunity to develop fire support coordination skills.	6
The opportunity to exercise on a range facility with simulated enemy positions, fortifications and obstacles.	7
The opportunity to conduct maneuver with live fire assets.	8

Table 3. Relative Importance of Live Fire Exercise Benefits

Chart 2 plots the effectiveness of Range 400 in providing benefits against the relative importance of those benefits. In effect, Chart 2 compares Chart 1 and Table 2. A truly effective training method would have a strong correlation between effectiveness and importance. This relationship would mean that the facility performs its most important functions more effectively than functions of lesser importance. This correlation would be illustrated by points plotted in the extreme upper left quandrant of Chart 2. In the case of Range 400 we can see that the two most important traits (stressful environment and real-time decision making) only correspond to effectiveness scores of 4. In the opinion of the participants, Range 400's most important traits are not its most effective traits.

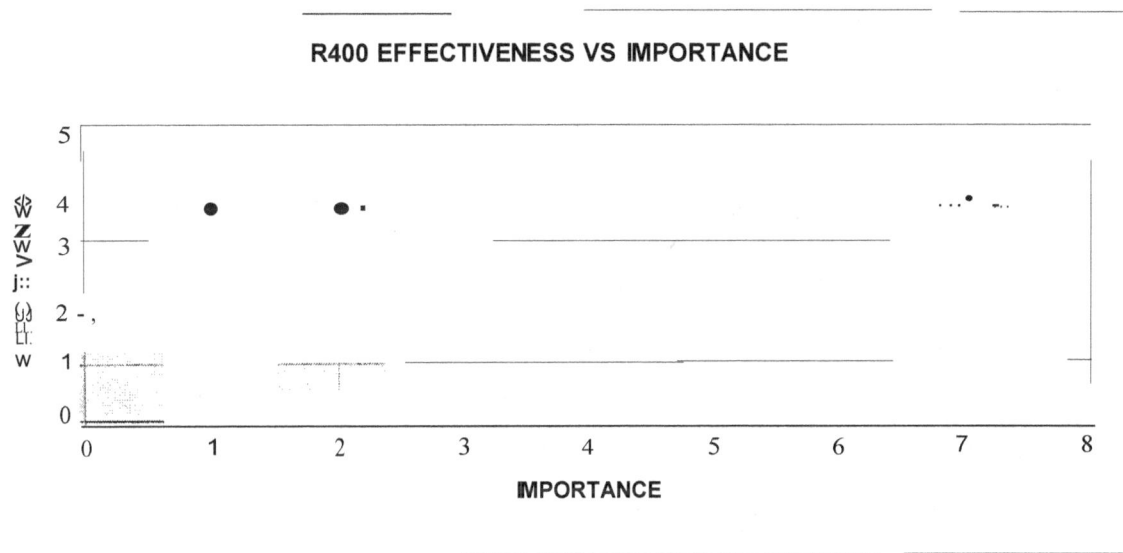

R400 EFFECTIVENESS VS IMPORTANCE

Chart 2. Range 400 Effectiveness Vs. Importance

3.   Assess **Perceived Limitations of R400.**

Chart 3 illustrates the perceived limitations of Range 400 by the subject matter experts. The values in Chart 3 represent the median values of the participanf s opinions and summarize data from Appendix C. The numbers on the left side of the chart correspond to Questions 13-18 in Appendix A.

As can be seen the strongest opinions relate to Question 13 (an unresponsive and static enemy force). Additionally; (Question 14), the lack of objective feedback, (Question 15), lack of simulated friendly casualties and (Question 16), the inability to reconstruct the exercise were also strongly identified.

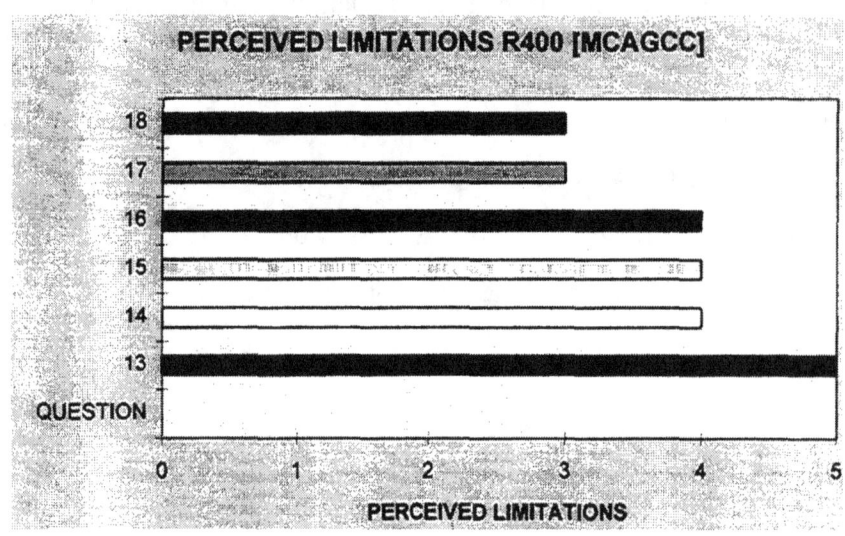

Chart 3. Perceived Limitations of Range 400

4. Rank Limitations of USMC Live Fire Training

Table 4 illustrates the participant's opinion on the items that impact adversely on USMC live fire training. The scores were compiled by taking the median value of all of the rankings (Question 19, Appendix A), and then sorting them from lowest (most important) to highest (least important). Ties were broken where possible by looking at the mean ranking for that question. The lack of realistic and interactive enemy forces is identified as having the most significant impact on the effectiveness of live fire training. Limited objective feedback and safety constraints were also identified as having significant adverse impact on the effectiveness of live fire training.

TRAIT	RANK
Realistic and interactive enemy forces	1
Limited feedback on weapons employment.	2
Safety Constraints.	3
Availability of adequate range facilities	4
Material Constraints	5
Limited ability to reconstruct/replay the exercise	6

Table 4. Relative Importance of Live Fire Limitations

B.   LEATHERNET

1.   Assess **Leathernet's Perceived Benefits**

Chart 4 illustrates the opinions of the subject matter experts on the effectiveness of LeatherNet in providing certain benefits to company and platoon commanders. The values in Chart 4 represent the median values of the participant's opinions. The numbers on the left side of the chart correspond to Questions 4-11 in Appendix D. The data for Chart 4 can be found in Appendix E.

Analysis of Chart 4 reveals that the subject matter experts feel that LeatherNet is effective in providing the following: (Question 7), an opportunity to develop fire support skills, (Question 8), an opportunity to coordinate maneuver with fire support, (Question 9), an opportunity to be evaluated by experts outside your chain of command, (Question 10), an opportunity to exercise on a facility that includes simulated enemy and (Question 11), the opportunity to make decisions in a real time scenario.

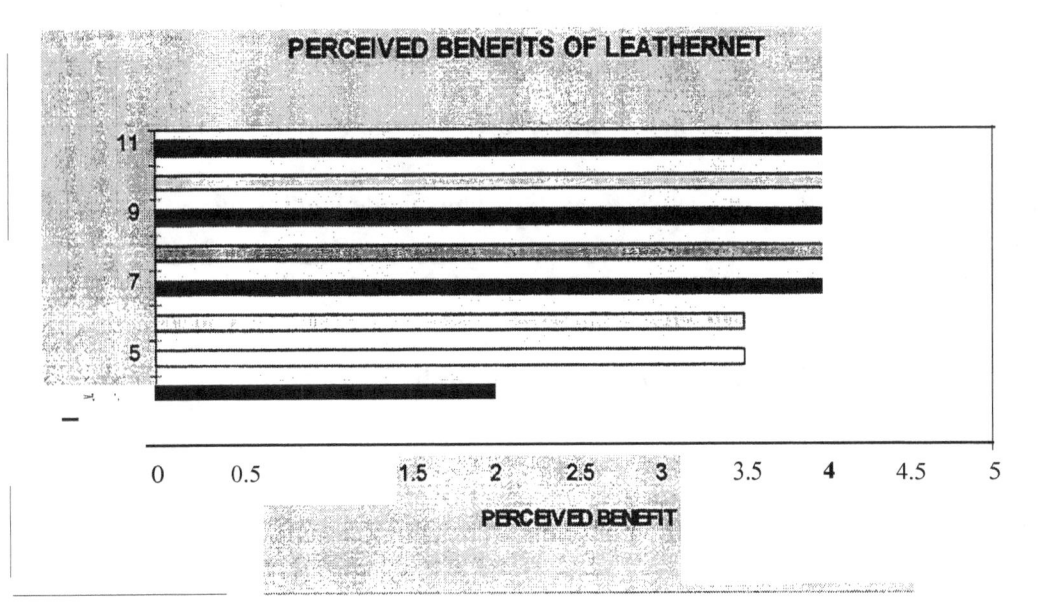

Chart 4. Perceived Effectiveness of Leathernet

45

2. Rank Traits of Leathernet

Table 5 illustrates the opinion of the subject matter experts regarding the relative importance of certain traits desired in a simulator like LeatherNet. The scores were compiled by taking the median value of all of the rankings (Question 12, Appendix D), and then sorting them from lowest (most important) to highest (least important). Ties were broken where possible by looking at the mean ranking for that question. The most important trait identified is the opportunity to exercise on a facility that includes simulated enemy positions, the second most important trait is the opportunity to exercise tactical decision skills in a real time environment.

TRAIT	RANK
An opportunity to exercise your unit on range facility that includes simulated enemy positions, fortifications and obstacles	1
An opportunity to exercise tactical decisionmaking skills in a real time scenario.	2
An opportunity to develop, evaluate and refine maneuver skills.	3
An opportunity to plan for and execute an operation with combined arms live fire assets.	4.5
An opportunity to develop, evaluate and refine fire support control skills.	4.5
An opportunity to be evaluated by subject matter experts outside of your chain of command	6
An opportunity to coordinate the maneuver of tactical units while employing live fire assets	7
An opportunity to perform in a stressful environment that realistically simulates combat	8

Table 5. Relative Importance of Desired Traits

Chart 5 plots the effectiveness of LeatherNet against the relative importance of desired traits. While LeatherNet did not receive any median scores of 5, it shows that the most effective traits of LeatherNet correlate to the most important traits.

3. Assess **Leathernet's Perceived Ability To Enhance R400**

Chart 6 illustrates the subject matter expert's opinion regarding LeatherNet's ability to enhance Range 400 exercises. The values in Chart 6 represent the median values of the participant's opinions. The numbers on the left side of the chart correspond to Questions 13-20 in Appendix D. The data for Chart 6 can be found in Appendix E.

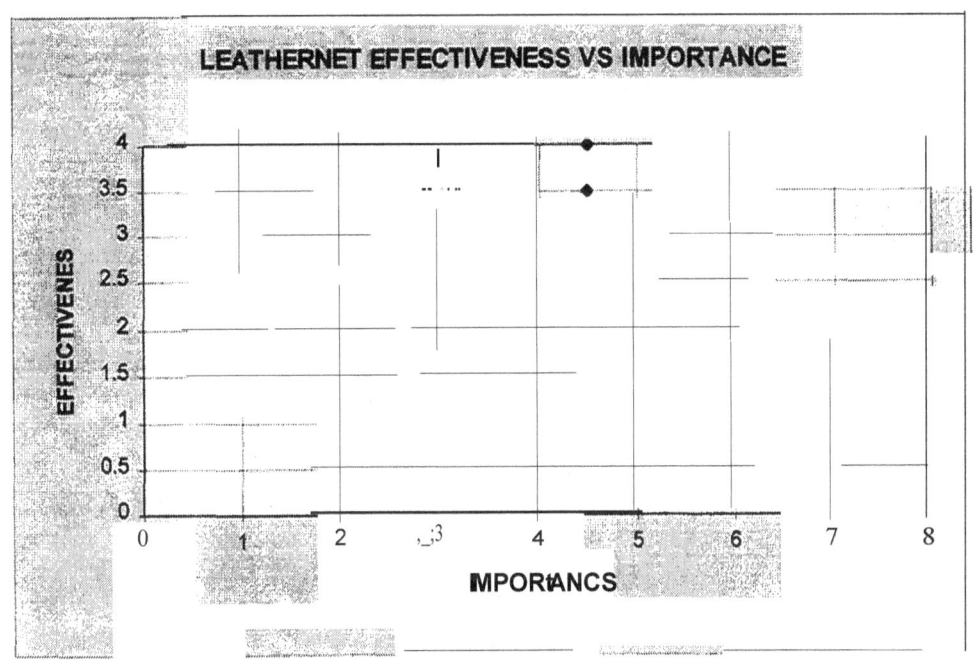

Chart 5. Effectiveness Versus Importance

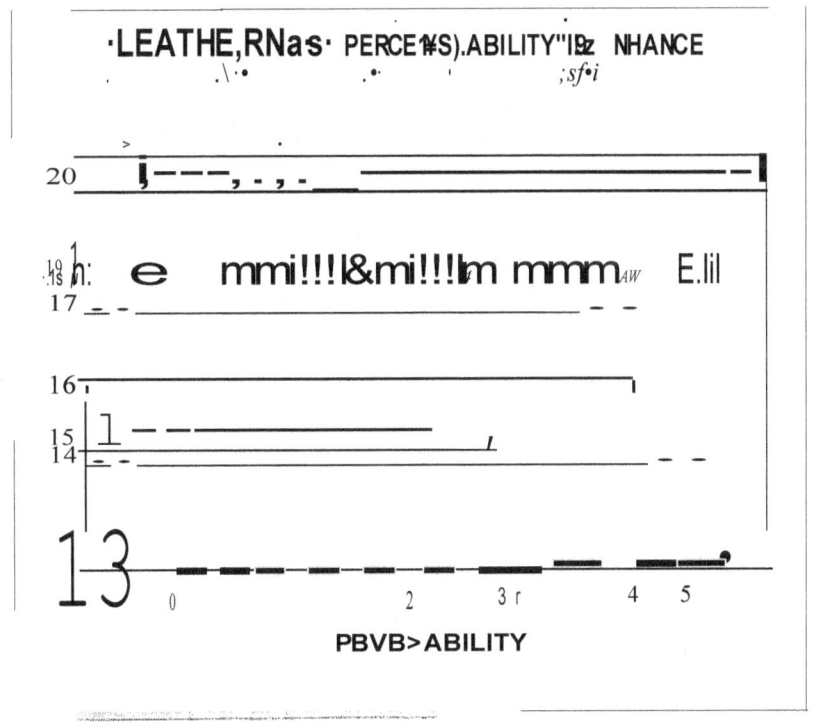

Chart 6. Leathernet's Ability to Enhance Range 400

Analysis of this data reveals that LeatherNet is capable of enhancing Range 400 by providing a more responsive and interactive enemy force and providing the ability to conduct this type of training at another location.

4. Rank Leathernet's Perceived Abilities to Overcome Limitations of Live Fire Training

Table 6 illustrates the opinion of the subject matter experts regarding the relative effectiveness of LeatherNet in overcoming the limitations of Marine Corps live fire exercises. The scores were compiled by taking the median value of all of the rankings (Question 18, Appendix E), and then sorting them from lowest (most important) to highest (least important). Ties were broken where possible by looking at the mean ranking for that question.

Analysis of Table 6 indicates that LeatherNet is most effective in providing the ability to conduct a *more* detailed playback and debrief of the exercise. The second most effective trait is the ability to provide a realistic enemy force.

TRAIT	RANK
Providing the ability to conduct a *more* detailed playback and debrief of the exercise.	1
Providing a more responsive and interactive enemy force that behaves realistically.	2
Providing an opportunity for commanders to control their units and simultaneously evaluate their subordinate's performance	3
Providing for realistic simulated friendly casualties.	4
Providing objective, quantitative feedback on the effectiveness of your fire support plan.	5
The ability to conduct the *same exercise* under varying conditions, or with a modified plan and evaluate the outcome.	6
The ability to conduct this training aboard ship, or at another location (CLNC?).	7
The ability to conduct danger close fire support in a safe environment.	8

Table 6. Relative Effectiveness of Leathernet in Overcoming Limitations Related to Live Fire Training

Chart 7 compares the subject matter expert's opinion on the effectiveness of Range 400 with the effectiveness of LeatherNet. This data compares Questions 4-11 of Appendix A with Questions 4-11 of Appendix D. Analysis of this data reveals that Range 400 is tlhe more effective training tool in several categories. However. the experts feel that LeatherNet is equally effective in providing an opportunity to be evaluated by experts outside of your chain of command, an opportunity to exercise on a facility with simulated enemy fortifications and the ability to exercise tactical decisionrnaking skills in a real-time environment. Chart 7 indicates only one trait where LeatherNet does not provide the benefit and that is the opportunity to perform in a stressful environment that realistically simulates combat.

BENEFITS

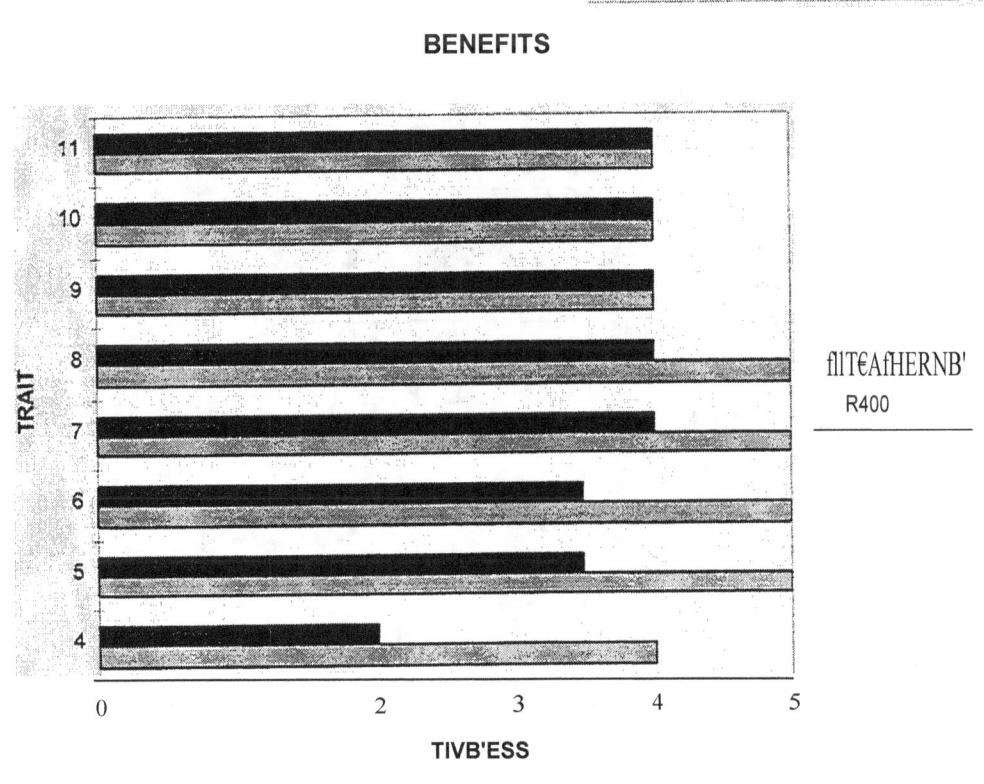

Chart 7. Comparison of Effectiveness

5. **Assess Leathernet's Ability to Fulfill Marine Corps Modeling and Simulation End States**

Chart 8 illustrates the subject matter expert's opinion regarding LeatherNet's ability to fulfill the Marine Corps desired modeling and simulation end states. The values in Chart 8 represent the median values of the participant's opinions. The numbers on the left side of the chart correspond to Questions 22-27 in Appendix D. The data for Chart 8 can be found in Appendix E.

Analysis of Chart 8 reveals that the experts feel that LeatherNet is capable of fulfilling many of the desired modeling and simulation end states. The capability of LeatherNet to be used in the acquisition process is the only end state that experts did not agree on.

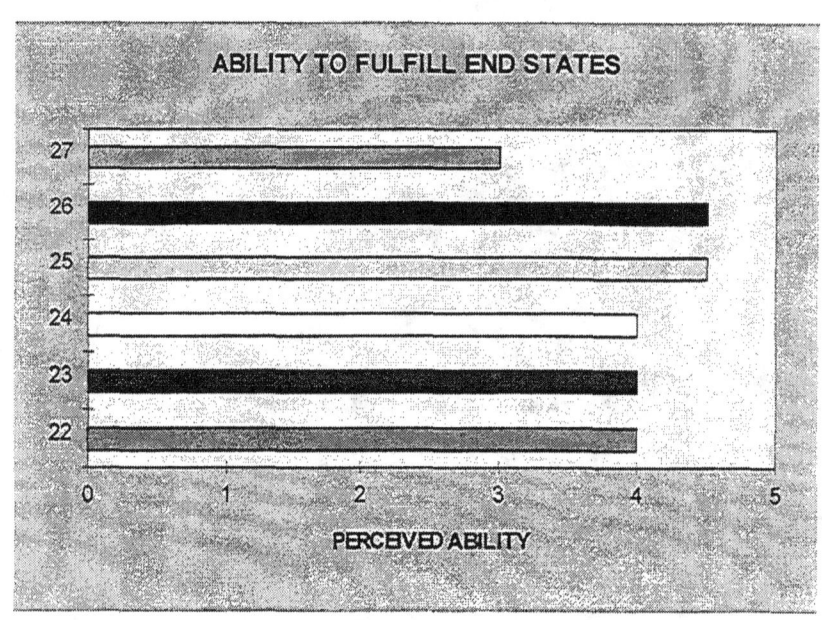

Chart 8. Leathernet's Ability to Fulfill the Desired End States

6. **Assess Participant's Comments**

a. *Effectiveness of LeatherNet*

The subject matter experts identified several other areas where LeatherNet may provide effective training for company and platoon commanders. Some of the highlights were:

50

- LeatherNet would be an effective tool to refresh commanders who have been out of their MOS for long periods of time.

- Gives commanders a chance to experiment with new tactical concepts without the requirement of troops in the field.

- LeatherNet would provide effective training for LAV and armor platoon commanders.

- LeatherNet would be a good tool for conducting mission rehearsal as well as tactical decision games.

   b.   *Leathernet's Ability to Enhance Marine Corps Live Fire Training*

Subject matter experts identified the following items as additional ways that LeatherNet could enhance live fire training.

- Identify and analyze potential fratricide situations.

- LeatherNet seems more effective at simulating large scale exercises than small scale exercises.

- LeatherNet would be useful in the development and evaluation of unit standard operating procedures.

   c.   *What was most impressive about this simulator?*

The following is a summary of expert's responses:

- The ability to view a battlefield from different views.

- Graphic representation of troops and terrain.

- The ability to respond to voice commands.

- The ability to replay the situation exactly how it occurred.

- The interaction of enemy and friendly forces.

   d.   *What was least impressive about this simulator?*

The following is a summary of expert's responses:

- Lack of basic "common sense" behavior by Semi-Autonomous Forces. Enemy squad did not occupy trenchline and base of fire's continuous engagement of objective.

- Amount of user expertise required to interface with the system.

- Doesn't create stress.

e. *What type of objective measures would be useful?*

The following is a summary of expert's responses:

- Ammunition expenditure.
- Percentage of time that maneuver units are exposed to enemy observation, direct fire.

C. DISCUSSION

The results of this evaluation are generally positive in regards to LeatherNet's ability. While the subject matter experts were not universally impressed, they did recognize the capability of LeatherNet to enhance traditional training methods. Considering that LeatherNet is less than half-way through its development, this degree of acceptance is encouraging.

The most significant finding is that LeatherNet's most effective capability (providing a realistic and responsive enemy force) is also considered to be the greatest deficiency of Range 400.

The one capability of LeatherNet that was not accepted by the subject matter experts was the capability to replicate the stress of a realistic combat situation. Some of the subject matter experts commented that stress could only be achieved in a field environment. However, it should be noted that stress can be created by a simulator when the participant is forced to make decisions in the face of uncertainty. Since the participants of this evaluation only observed the demonstration they did not get a good appreciation of this attribute.

Due to heavy operational commitments within the 7th Marine Regiment, several of the proposed participants backed out at the last minute. Therefore, there was a much smaller group of participants available. More significantly, several of the participants were relatively inexperienced. The median time in service was only three years, and none had served in combat. Only one participant had experience as a company commander and his responses show a much higher acceptance of LeatherNet than the other members of the group. [Appendix E, Column 3]

Some of the evaluator's comments were biased by the fact that MC SAF behavior is not completely developed. The fact that the defenders did not occupy their trenchline was mentioned by several members of the group. Additionally, the fact that the base of fire continually suppressed the enemy for over twenty minutes is really a criticism of the demonstration rather than the simulator, but that evaluator felt that it detracted from the simulation. More realistic ammunition limitations can be built into LeatherNet exercises but were not considered for this demonstration.

V. SUMMARY AND RECOMMENDATIONS

A.   THE MARINE CORPS OF THE FUTURE

The security needs of the nation dictate that the Marine Corps be a responsive, flexible force that can react quickly to a wide variety of threats. Maintaining well trained forces that operate effectively in joint and combined operations is essential. Developing and implementing new concepts like Operational Maneuver From the Sea are critical to effectively serving the future needs of the nation. However, in this period of fiscal drought, the implementation of new concepts and the maintenance of high state of readiness require innovative and novel solutions.

The Marine Corps has stated both its intention and strategy to maximize the effectiveness of its forces by the use of modeling and simulation. By committing to the development of effective simulation products now, the Marine Corps will receive significant dividends as these technologies mature.

B.   TRAINING EFFECTIVENESS EVALUATIONS

The evaluation of the effectiveness of training alternatives in DOD is not a well developed science. It is not practical to attempt to evaluate the effectiveness of a simulator without a proven method of evaluating the training alternative that it is meant to replace or augment. This is especially true when considering the effectiveness of collective training of such units as Marine Air Ground Task Force staffs.

C.   CAPABILITIES OF LEATHERNET

LeatherNet is designed to demonstrate the potential of modeling and simulation technology in training Marines to fight. While it has great potential as a training tool for Marine commanders and their staffs, its most significant benefit is its ability to demonstrate the value of simulation in training, mission planning and rehearsal.

1.   Current Status

Still in the early phases of development, LeatherNet has not yet achieved its full potential. Despite its current limited functionality, it demonstrates the potential to enhance Marine Corps training in several areas. This evaluation demonstrated the ability of LeatherNet to provide a responsive and interactive enemy and to provide more useful feedback on weapons employment. This is significant because subject matter experts identified those particular traits as the most important limitations of Marine Corps live fire training.

Subject matter experts identified unrealistic or incomplete Semi-Autonomous Force behavior as the least impressive feature of LeatherNet. As knowledge acquisition and engineering efforts continue one could expect to see an improvement in these types of behaviors. The involvement of Marine subject matter experts is essential to this process.

Subject matter experts did not feel that LeatherNet could create a stressful environment that realistically simulates combat. This trait was also identified as being one of the most important traits of Marine Corps training. It should be noted that this evaluation was based on a demonstration where the experts only observed a single user create a tactical scenario and let it run its course. The evaluators in this case did not have the opportunity to make tactical decisions in the face of uncertainty. Had the experts actually used the system and had the opportunity to make those kinds of decisions, their opinions may have been different.

Subject matter experts also felt that the system required a great deal of user expertise. However, the author had only a one hour orientation by the System engineer and was able to utilize almost all functions of LeatherNet with minimal problems. It seems reasonable that most Marine Corps officers with even minimal computer skills could learn to use this system. A user manual is being developed and this should provide additional assistance.

2.   Expected Potential

Subject matter experts felt that LeatherNet is capable of fulfilling many of the Marine Corps' desired modeling and simulation end states. Considering that the subject matter experts saw a very limited demonstration of LeatherNet's potential, the degree of acceptance was, in the author's opinion, significant.

LeatherNet's primary goal is not to fulfill specific Marine Corps needs, but rather demonstrate the potential of this technology. As the Marine Corps component of STOW 97, LeatherNet will demonstrate the utility of large scale joint simulated exercises. The lessons learned from STOW 97 will help to guide DOD in the development of a world class simulation environment.

Despite the fact that it is only a demonstration of technology, LeatherNet will benefit the Marine Corps in many ways. As a training tool, it has the potential to enhance traditional training methods by allowing leaders to operate against a responsive and interactive enemy in a realistic environment. Additionally, it will expose a great number of Marines to the potential capability of this technology for mission planning, briefing and rehearsal.

LeatherNet will continue to mature and evolve throughout the next few years. LeatherNet's final version will represent a set of core-capabilities that will evolve into Marine Corps simulators of the future. These capabilities represent a stepping stone to the operational systems that will fulfill the Marine Corps' envisioned modeling and simulation end states.

D.   RECOMMENDED ACTION

The Marine Corps must be an active participant m the development and evaluation of LeatherNet to fully reap its benefits. The strategic vision outlined in the Marine Corps Modeling and Simulation Masterplan is the correct first step, but vision is not enough. The Marine Corps must develop the specific guidance that prioritizes the efforts related to LeatherNet.

DOD experience with simulators shows that the most successful simulators had a high degree of user acceptance, a well developed training plan to show how the simulator should be used, acceptable costs, and minimal interference with traditional training methods. Marine Corps utilization of LeatherNet must consider those factors.   [Ref. 26]

1.   Development of Littoral Areas Terrain Data Base

The terrain data base that LeatherNet uses is Marine Corps Air Ground Combat Center. Given the importance of combined arms training in the Marine Corps, this is an appropriate place to start. However, most Marine Corps operations occur in the littoral areas of the world. Therefore, the Marine Corps should pursue the development of littoral area terrain data bases to conduct mission planning and rehearsal for amphibious operations. This area is currently receiving little attention, and the Marine Corps must champion its development. Successful implementation of new concepts such as Operational Maneuver from the Sea will depend on the development of high resolution models of the amphibious environment. [Ref. 36]

2.   Cooperation with USNillOD

DOD is steadily moving closer to a joint environment for operations, training and support. The Marine Corps has much to gain by cooperating with the other services in the development of modeling and simulation products. Interoperability is obviously a major concern in Distributed Interactive Simulations and Marine Corps simulators must meet these standards. More importantly, it is necessary for the Marine Corps to ensure that representations of Marine forces are accurately portrayed in all DOD simulations. This will demonstrate the unique capabilities of Marine forces to the other services and insure that Marine forces are employed according to doctrine.

3.   Development of a Utilization Plan for LeatherNet

Distributed Interactive Simulation systems are developing rapidly and demonstrate immense potential to improve unit training and effectiveness in a wide variety of applications. However, the development of training strategies, i.e. ways to use Distributed Interactive Simulation systems to improve training is lagging behind the development of the actual technology. The question of how to most effectively use this technology will be a major concern. Meaningful tests to evaluate the cost and training effectiveness of systems will be a major undertaking, but are necessary to optimize the use of the simulator. [Ref. 26]

The Marine Corps should devote significant resources to the development of evaluation methodologies of training alternatives to determine the optimal combination of simulator training and traditional methods. Once systems like LeatherNet are properly evaluated, a utilization plan should be developed to optimize its strengths as a training tool.

4. Development of Communications Network

A stand-alone system located at Marine Corps Air Ground Combat Center will provide only limited value to the Marine Corps. The need for Marine units from other locations to use this system is critical. The Marines' major operational forces reside at locations other than Marine Corps Air Ground Combat Center and would greatly benefit from the opportunity to use this system. Furthermore, the capability to remotely train on this system could result in significant cost avoidance by reducing the number of forces that must be transported to Marine Corps Air Ground Combat Center.

5. Educate Marines on Modeling and Simulation

For this system to be truly effective, it must have the confidence of the users in the fleet. Resistance to new technology is always a consideration, and Marines are no exception. It is therefore imperative that a comprehensive education program be developed to inform Marines of the capabilities of systems like LeatherNet. This education should not attempt the "hard sell" of a system's capabilities, but an honest assessment by Marines who have used the system. Documents such as the Modeling and Simulation MasterPlan and Modeling and Simulation Investment Plan should receive the widest dissemination and this has not yet happened.

Providing Marines with the opportunity to use the system and recording their impressions will also be beneficial. Frequent demonstrations that could be recorded on video would also be effective in the education process.

E.   ADJUSTMENTS TO METHODOLOGY

The methodology for this evaluation was heavily constrained by time and resources. A more detailed evaluation with a larger and more diverse group of participants would lend more credibility to the results.

1.   Lessons Learned

The evaluation that was conducted demonstrated several lessons about conducting this type of research. The most significant finding is that participants who only observe a demonstration get a limited exposure to the capabilities of the system. Specifically, the participants in this exercise did not have the opportunity to make the kind of decisions that would normally be made in the traditional training environment (i.e., how to react to an unpredictable situation and engage enemy forces). This prevented them from gaining a complete appreciation of the systems capabilities.

It is difficult to get genuine subject matter experts to participate in these type of evaluations without command sponsorship. Participants for this evaluation were lined up several weeks in advance through personal contacts at Marine Corps Air Ground Combat Center. However, the heavy operational tempo in 7th Marines caused several last minute substitutions and no shows. This resulted in a group of evaluators with somewhat limited experience.

Participants in this type of evaluation need a solid understanding of Marine Corps modeling and simulation issues. Most of the participants were uninformed as to the desired modeling and simulation end states or the principles behind Distributed Interactive Simulation. A short background brief prior to the evaluation is not sufficient.

2.   Recommendations

Have participants actually use the system. This requires supervised training and the development of a scenario that will force them to use their tactical decision making skills.

Get command sponsorship. Unless these evaluations have the support of Marine Corps Modeling And Simulation Management Office and the Commanding General of Marine Corps Air Ground Combat Center, participation will not be a high priority.

Insure that participants are well versed in modeling and simulation issues. It is not necessary for them to understand the technical principles of Distributed Interactive Simulation, but familiarity with the concept is essential.

F.   AREAS FOR FURTHER RESEARCH

There is a great deal of further research that can be done with regard to LeatherNet. A similar evaluation on a larger scale should be done with the changes in methodology suggested above. The capabilities of LeatherNet will be continually improving with time, it would be interesting to track changes in user's perceptions of its capabilities.

Developing methodologies to evaluate the effectiveness of collective training is vital to optimal utilization of simulators that support that training. Research to study the effectiveness of training at Marine Corps Air Ground Combat Center would be especially helpful.

Once proper evaluation methodologies of training alternatives are developed, an experiment to measure the effectiveness of LeatherNet could then be conducted. Marine units training at Marine Corps Air Ground Combat Center could be randomly assigned to control and experimental groups. Both groups could conduct identical training exercises that are critiqued by Tactical Exercise Evaluation and Control Group (TEECG). The commanders and staff of the experimental group then conduct training sessions with LeatherNet. The control group would use map or sand-table exercises. Both groups would then be evaluated on a second exercise. This experiment would illustrate the training effectiveness of LeatherNet as compared to traditional training methods.

LIST OF REFERENCES

1. Kitfield, James, *Trading Bullets for Bytes,* Government Executive, June, 1994.

2. United States Marine Corps, *Concepts and Issues,* 1994.

3. United States Marine Corps, *Marine Air-Ground Task Force Master Plan 1990-2000,* 1993.

4. O'Keefe, Sean G., Kelso, Frank B., Admiral, USN, and Mundy, Carl E., General USMC, *From the Sea: A New Direction for the Naval Services,* Marine Corps Gazette, November, 1992.

5. United States General Accounting Office, National Security Issues, Report No. GAO/OCG-93-9TR, December, 1993.

6. McKenzie, Kenneth F., Major, USMC, *The Marine Corps of Tomorrow,* U.S. Naval Institute Proceedings, November 1993.

7. Lawson, Chris, *Battle for 12 ARGs,* Navy Times, August 22, 1994.

8. United States Marine Corps, <u>Operational Maneuver from the Sea</u>, 1992.

9. Mazarr, Michael, et. al., *The Military Technical Revolution, A Structual Famework,* Center For Strategic and International Studies, March 1993.

10. Goure', Daniel, *The Military Technical Revolution,* Army Research and Acquisition Bulletin, January-February, 1994.

11. United States Marine Corps, *Marine Corps Modeling and Simulation Master Plan* (Draft), 1994.

12. Herskovitz, Don, *Military Computing in the Year 2001 and Beyond,* Journal of Electronic Defense, February 1994.

13. Hoffman, F.G., Major, USMCR, *Training 2001,* Marine Corps Gazette, July, 1994.

14. DIS Steering Committee, Institute for Simulation and Training, *The DIS Vision (Comment Draft),* October, 1993.

15. DIS HOMEPAGE, URL: http://www.tiig.ist.ucf.edu/ms_web/papers/dis_paper/dis.html", May, 1994.

16. Lynn, L., Advanced Research Projects Agency, *Statement before the Subcommitte on National Security, House Appropriations Committee,* March, 1993.

17. Defense Modeling and Simulation Office, *Defense Modeling and Simulation Initivative,* May,1992.

18. United States Marine Corps, OH 2, <u>The Marine Air-Ground Task Force,</u> March, 1987.

19. Krolak, C. C., General, United States Marine Corps, Commandant's Planning Guidance, July, 1995.

20. Armed Forces Communications and Electronics Association, *Evolutionary Acquistion Study,* June, 1993.

21. Office of Technology Assessment, Congress of the United States, *Virtual Reality and Technologiesfor Combat Simulation,* June, 1994.

22. Garrett, R. G., *ADS: Looking Toward the Future,* PHALANX, The Bulletin of Military Operations Research, June, 1995.

23. O'Byme, E. C., Major, USMC, *Advanced Distributed Simulation,* Marine Corps Gazette, July, 1994.

24. Perla, P. P., *Future Directions for Wargaming,* Joint Forces Quarterly, Summer, 1994.

25. Office of the Under Secretary of Defense Personnel and Readiness, *Use of Simulation in DOD Training,* Report to the House Committee on National Securtiy and Senate Armed Forces Committee, April, 1995.

26. Orlansky, J., et. al., Institute for Defense Analysis, *The Value of Simulation For Training,* September, 1994.

27. Dewar, J., et al., Rand Corporation, *Credible Uses of the Distributed Interactive Simulation (DIS) System* October 1994.

28. Kincaid, P., *Development of a Military Standardfor Cost and Training Efectiveness,* Institute for Simulation and Training, September 1993.

29. Proceedings, Issues of Militray Cost/Training Effectiveness, Symposium at the 14th Interservice/Industry Training Systems and Education Conference, November,1992.

30. Andrews, D. H., Air Force, CTEA Programs, Proceedings, Issues of Military Cost/ Training Effectiveness, Symposium at the 14th Interservice/Industry Training Systems and Education Conference, November,1992.

31. Simpson, H., Defense Manpower Data Center, *Cost-Effectiveness Analysis of Training in the Department of Defense,* June, 1995.

32. Burnside, Billy L., United States Army Research Institute for the Behavioral and Social Sciences Research Report 1565, *Assessing the Capabilites of Training Simulations: A Method and Simulation Networking (SIMNET) Application,* June, 1990.

33. Schwab, J. R., *Concept Evaluation Program of Simulaiton Networking,* March, 1988.

34. Adams, Steven R., and Lind, Judith H., *Team Tactical Engagement Simulator (TTES): Perceived Training Value,* December, 1994.

35. Advanced Projects Research Agency, *Leathernet Vision Statement and Integrated Project Plan,* 1994.

36. Untied States Marine Corps, *Marine Corps Modeling and Simulation Investment Plan,* April, 1995.

APPENDIX A. RANGE **400** ASSESSMENT

From: Major John F. Kelly USMC

To: _____

Subj.: Range 400 Assessment.

Fellow Marine,

The purpose of this questionnaire is to gather opinions on the effectiveness of live fire training in the Marine Corps. I am specifically interested in your assessment of benefits and limitations of the Range 400 exercise at MCAGCC, 29 Palms. This questionnaire will be used as part of my thesis research which seeks to determine the potential capabilities of simulation to _enhance_ live fire training.

Please return the completed questionnaire to Major John F. Kelly, PM-41(SMC 2723) in the envelope provided NLT_____. If you have any questions or further comments feel free to contact me: **Voicemail: DSN 878-2536, X-2723 or at 599 E Michelson Rd. Monterey. Ca., 93040.** Thank you for your cooperation.

Semper Fi,

John F. Kelly
Major, USMC

1. Please indicate your Time in Service._____

2. Have you served in combat? (Circle One)   Yes   No

3. Please indicate the number of times that you have participated in a Live Fire exercise on Range 400 as a:

        A. Rifle Platoon Commander
        B. Weapons Platoon Commander
        C. Company Commander
        D. Evaluator (TEECG)
        E. Other (Please describe)

In answering questions 4-11, please circle the number that best corresponds to your opinion.
Use the following code to indicate your answer:
    1. Strongly Disagree.
    2. Disagree.
    3. No Opinion.
    4. Agree.
    5. Strongly Agree.

Range 400 exercises are effective in training <u>platoon and</u> company commanders by providing:

4. An opportunity to perform in a stressful environment that realistically simulates combat.

       1   2   3   4   5

5. An opportunity to plan for and execute an operation with combined arms live fire assets.

       1   2   3   4   5

6. An opportunity to develop, evaluate and refine maneuver skills.

       1   2   3   4   5

7. An opportunity to develop, evaluate and refine fire support control skills.

       1   2   3   4   5

8. An opportunity to coordinate the maneuver of tactical units while employing live fire assets.

          1   2   3   4   5

9. An opportunity to be evaluated by subject matter experts outside of your chain of command.

          1   2   3   4   5

10. An opportunity to exercise your unit on range facility that includes simulated enemy positions, fortifications and obstacles.

          1   2   3   4   5

11. An opportunity to exercise tactical decisionmaking skills in a real time scenario.

          1   2   3   4   5

12 Please rank the following items according to their importance in Marine Corps live fire training. (1 for the most important benefit, 8 for the least important benefit.)

    A. Stressful environment that realistically simulates combat.
    B. The opportunity to work with combined arms assets on one range.
    C. The opportunity to develop maneuver skills.
    D. The opportunity to develop fire support coordination skills.
    E. The opportunity to conduct maneuver with live fire assets.
    F. The opportunity to be evaluated by experts outside your chain of command.
    G. The opportunity to exercise on a range facility with simulated enemy positions, fortifications and obstacles.
    H. The opportunity to exercise tactical decision-making skills in a real time scenario.

Please use this space to list any other benefits that you feel Range 400 may provide to Company

and Platoon Commanders.

_____

_____

_____

_____

In answering questions 13-19, please circle the number that best corresponds to your opinion.
Use the following code to indicate your answer:

1. Strongly Disagree.
2. Disagree.
3. No Opinion.
4. Agree.
5. Strongly Agree.

Range 400 exercises are currently limited by the foilowing

factors:

13. An unresponsive and static enemy force that does not behave realistically.

       1   2   3   4   5

14. A lack of objective, quantitative (i.e. % of time that enemy is successfully suppressed) feedback on the effectiveness of your fire support plan.

       1   2   3   4   5

15. A lack of realistic simulated friendly casualties.

                  2   3   4   5

16. An inability to conduct a detailed playback and debrief of the exercise.

       1   2   3   4   5

17. A lack of opportunity for commanders to control their units and simultaneously evaluate their subordinate's performance.

       1   2   3   4   5

18. The inability to conduct the *same exercise* under varying conditions, or with a modified plan and evaluate the outcome.

       1   2   3   4   5

19. Please rank the following items according to their impact on the effectiveness of Marine Corps live fire training. (1 for the most limiting factor, 6 for the least limiting factor.)

   A. Safety Constraints
   B. Material Constraints (Ammo, personnel etc.)
   C. Limited Feedback on effectiveness of weapons employment
   D. Limited ability to reconstruct/replay exercise for detailed debrief.
   E. Realistic and interactive enemy forces.
   F. Availability of adequate range facilities.

Please use this space to list any other factors that you consider to be a limitation of Marine Corps live fire training.

_____

_____

_____

_____

_____

20.   Please indicate your familiarity with computers.(1 not familiar, 5 being extremely familiar)

        1   2   3   4   5

21.   Please indicate your confidence in computers to assist in training Marines. (1 indicating no confidence, 5 indicating extreme confidence)

        1   2   3   4   5

Thank you again for your cooperation. Please return this questionnaire to Major John F. Kelly.

APPENDIX B. RANGE 400 ASSESSMENT DATA
(Naval Postgraduate School (NPS))

1	TIME IN SERVICE		15	8	13	12	5	4
2	COMBAT		0	1	1	0	0	0
3	A		0	0	0	10	0	0
	8		0	0	0	5	0	0
	C		2	0	1	3	0	0
	D		15	10	1	0	0	0
	E		0	10	0	0	1	1
4			3	4	4	5	5	3
5			4	5	4	5	5	5
6			5	4	4	1	5	4
7			4	4	4	5	5	5
8			5	4	5	5	5	5
9			4	5	4	4	5	4
10			5	4	4	5	5	5
11			5	4	4	4	2	4
12	A		1	3	5	5	1	4
	8		4	1	3	8	3	7
	C		6	6	4	4	5	5
	D		5	4	2	1	4	3
	E		3	2	1	2	2	2
	F		8	8	7	7	8	8
	G		7	7	6	6	6	6
	H		2	5	8	3	7	1
13			4	4	3	2	5	5
14			5	5	2	5	4	5
15			5	3	3	5	5	5
16			4	3	3	5	2	5
17			2	2	3	1	1	5
18			4	4	3	1	4	2
19	A		6	6	4	1	4	5
	8		5	3	2	6	5	4
	C		3	4	6	3	3	3
	D		2	5	3	5	6	2
	E		1	1	5	2	2	1
	F		4	2	1	4	1	6

75

APPENDIX B. RANGE 400 ASSESSMENT DATA
(Naval Postgraduate School (NPS))

13	14	15	12	7	118	10.72727	12
1	1	0	0	1	5		
0	0	0	0	1	11	1	0
1	0	0	1	1	8	0.727273	0
0	0	1	0	0	7	0.636364	0
0	0	0	0	0	26	2.363636	0
1	3	2	0	1	19	1.727273	1
2	4	3	2	4	39	3.545455	4
4	4	5	5	5	51	4.636364	5
4	3	3	5	4	42	3.818182	4
4	2	4	5	4	46	4.181818	4
4	4	4	4	5	50	4.545455	5
5	4	4	5	4	48	4.363636	4
4	5	4	5	5	51	4.636364	5
4	4	4	2	5	42	3.818182	4
1	5	4	8	1	38	3.454545	4
4	3	3	5	2	43	3.909091	3
8	6	6	4	5	59	5.363636	5
6	7	2	3	3	40	3.636364	3
3	1	1	2	4	23	2.090909	2
7	8	7	7	6	81	7.363636	7
5	2	8	6	7	66	6	6
2	4	5	1	8	46	4.181818	4
5	4	5	2	5	44	4	4
5	5	4	4	1	45	4.090909	5
4	2	2	1	1	36	3.272727	3
4	4	5	5	1	41	3.727273	4
4	3	2	4	1	28	2.545455	2
4	5	4	5	5	41	3.727273	4
1	6	1	1	1	36	3.272727	4
6	2	6	3	6	48	4.363636	5
4	4	2	2	4	38	3.454545	3
5	3	5	4	5	45	4.090909	5
2	5	4	5	2	30	2.727273	2
3	1	3	6	3	34	3.090909	3

APPENDIX C. RANGE 400 ASSESSMENT DATA
(Marine Corps Air Ground Combat Center)

NAME			1	2	3	4	5	SUM	MEDIAN
1 TIME IN SERVICE			15	3	18	2	2	40	3
2 COMBAT			0	0	0	0	0	0	
3 A			2	3	1	1	3	10	2
	B		0	2	0	0	0	2	0
	C		0	0	0	0	0	0	0
	D		0	0	25	0	0	25	0
	E		13	4	0	0	0	17	0
4			4	4	5	4	4	21	4
5			4	5	5	4	5	23	5
6			4	5	5	5	3	22	5
7			5	4	5	5	5	24	5
8			5	5	5	4	4	23	5
9			4	2	5	5	4	20	4
10			4	4	5	4	5	22	4
11			4	2	5	5	2	18	4
12 A			1	5	1	1	2	10	1
	B		5	1	3	8	5	22	5
	C		4	4	7	4	7	26	4
	D		6	6	4	5	3	24	5
	E		3	2	5	3	4	17	3
	F		8	7	8	7	8	38	8
	G		7	3	6	6	6	28	6
	H		2	8	2	2	1	15	2
13			5	3	5	5	5	23	5
14			5	4	4	5	2	20	4
15			5	2	3	5	4	19	4
16			4	2	4	4	2	16	4
17			2	2	4	3	4	15	3
18			2	1	5	5	3	16	3
19 A			6	2	6	3	2	19	3
	B		4	4	1	6	3	18	4
	C		3	1	4	2	6	16	3
	D		5	6	5	4	5	25	5
	E		2	3	3	1	1	10	2
	F		1	5	2	5	4	17	4
20			1	5	4	3	3	16	3
21			4	3	5	4	3	19	4

77

APPENDIX D. LEATHERNET ASSESSMENT

From: Major John F. Kelly USMC

To: —

Subj.: LeatherNet Assessment.

Fellow Marine,

The purpose of this questionnaire is to gather opinions on the effectiveness of simulation to *enhance* live fire training in the Marine Corps. I am specifically interested in your assessment of the capabilities of LeatherNet to *enhance* the training provide to Company and Platoon commanders conducting the Range 400 exercise at MCAGCC, 29 Palms. My research does not advocate the reduction in live fire training for Marines, but rather how we can get more value out of live fire training.

Please return the completed questionnaire to Major John F. Kelly before you leave today. If you have any questions or further comments feel free to contact me: or **Voicemail: DSN 878-2536. X-2723.** Thank you for your cooperation.

Semper Fi,

John F. Kelly
Major, USMC

In answering questions 4-11, please circle the number that best corresponds to your opinion. Use the following code to indicate your answer:

1. Strongly Disagree.
2. Disagree.
3. No Opinion.
4. Agree.
5. Strongly Agree.

LeatherNet exercises are effective in training <u>platoon and company commanders by providing:</u>

4.   An opportunity to perform in a stressful environment that realistically simulates combat.

        1   2   3   4   5

5.   An opportunity to plan for and execute an operation with combined arms live fire assets.

        1   2   3   4   5

6.   An opportunity to develop, evaluate and refine maneuver skills.

              2   3   4   5

7.   An opportunity to develop, evaluate and refine fire support control skills.

        1   2   3   4   5

8.   An opportunity to coordinate the maneuver of tactical units while employing live fire assets.

        1   2   3   4   5

9.   An opportunity to be evaluated by subject matter experts outside of your chain of command.

        1   2   3   4   5

10.   An opportunity to exercise your unit on range facility that includes simulated enemy positions, fortifications and obstacles.

        1   2   3   4   5

11. An opportunity to exercise tactical decision making skills in a real time scenario.

1   2   3   4   5

12. Please rank the following items according to their importance in Marine Corps live fire training. (1 for the most important benefit, 8 for the least important benefit.)

    A. Stressful environment that realistically simulates combat.
    B. The opportunity to work with combined arms assets on one range.
    C. The opportunity to develop maneuver skills.
    D. The opportunity to develop fire support coordination skills.
    E. The opportunity to conduct maneuver with live fire assets.
    F. The opportunity to be evaluated by experts outside your chain of command.
    G. The opportunity to exercise on a range facility with simulated enemy positions, fortifications and obstacles.
    H. The opportunity to exercise tactical decision-making skills in a real time scenario.

Please use this space to list any other benefits that you feel LeatherNet may provide to Company

and Platoon Commanders.

_____

_____

_____

_____

In answering questions 13-20, please circle the number that best corresponds to your opinion. Use the following code to indicate your answer:

1. **Strongly Disagree.**
2. **Disagree.**
3. **No Opinion.**
4. **Agree.**
5. **Strongly Agree.**

LeatherNet can enhance Range 400 exercises in the following areas:

13. Providing a more responsive and interactive enemy force that behaves realistically.

      1   2   3   4   5

14. Providing objective, quantitative (i.e. % of time that enemy is successfully suppressed) feedback on the effectiveness of your fire support plan.

      1   2   3   4   5

15. Providing for realistic simulated friendly casualties.

      1   2   3   4   5

16. Providing the ability to conduct a *more* detailed playback and debrief of the exercise.

      1   2   3   4   5

17. Providing an opportunity for commanders to control their units and simultaneously evaluate their subordinate's performance.

      1   2   3   4   5

18. The ability to conduct the *same exercise* under varying conditions, or with a modified plan and evaluate the outcome.

      1   2   3   4   5

19. The ability to conduct danger close fire support in a safe environment.

      1   2   3   4   5

20. The ability to conduct this training aboard ship, or at another location (CLNC?).

          1   2   3   4   5

21. Please rank the following items to indicate your opinion of the effectiveness of LeatherNet in overcoming limitations in live fire training. (1 to indicate the factor that LeatherNet is most effective in overcoming, 8 for the factor that LeatherNet is least effective in overcoming.)

    A. Realistic responsive enemy force
    B. Quantitative Feedback on effectiveness of weapons employment
    C. Simulated friendly casualty assessments
    D. Ability to reconstruct/replay exercise for detailed debrief
    E. Ability to evaluate subordinate's performance
    F. Ability to conduct the same exercise under varying conditions,
        or with a modified plan and evaluate the outcome
    G. Ability to conduct danger close fire support in training
    H. Availability of adequate range facilities

In answering questions 22-27, please circle the number that best corresponds to your opinion. Use the following code to indicate your answer:

    1. Strongly Disagree.
    2. Disagree.
    3. No Opinion.
    4. Agree.
    5. Strongly Agree. ·

22. LeatherNet demonstrates the capability to be an effective tool in training Company Commanders and their staffs.

          1   2   3   4   5

23. LeatherNet demonstrates the capability to be an effective Range 400 Mission Planning tool.

          1   2   3   4   5

24. LeatherNet demonstrates the capability to be an effective Range 400 Mission Rehearsal tool.

          1   2   3   4   5

25. LeatherNet demonstrates the capability to be an effective tool in evaluating tactical alternatives.

    1   2   3   4   5

26. LeatherNet demonstrates the capability to be an effective tool in evaluating Marine Corps requirements and doctrine.

    1   2   3   4   5

27. LeatherNet demonstrates the capability to be an effective tool in the acquisition process.

    1   2   3   4   5

Please use this space to list any other areas where you think that LeatherNet may be able to

enhance Marine Corps live fire training.

_____

_____

_____

_____

_____

What most impressed you about this simulator?

_____

_____

_____

What least impressed you about this simulator?

_____

_____

_____

What type of objective measures of effectiveness would you like to see in a simulator of this

type?

_____

_____

_____

_____

Thank you again for your cooperation. Please return this questionnaire to Major John F. Kelly

before you leave.

APPENDIX E. LEATHERNET ASSESSMENT DATA

NAME		1	2	3	4	5	SUM	MEDIAN
4		1	1	3	2	2	9	2
5		4	4	5	3	2	14	3.5
6		2	4	5	3	4	16	4
7		4	4	3	4	4	15	4
8		4	2	5	4	4	15	4
9		4	5	5	4	3	17	4.5
10		4	5	5	4	4	18	4.5
11		2	4	5	4	4	17	4
12	A	8	8	7	8	8	31	8
	B	3	5	3	4	5	17	4.5
	c	1	2	5	6	6	19	5.5
	D	2	6	4	5	4	19	4.5
	E	5	7	6	3	7	23	6.5
	F	6	4	8	7	3	22	5.5
	G	4	1	2	1	2	6	1.5
	H	7	3	1	2	1	7	1.5
13		4	5	5	5	5	20	5
14		4	5	5	5	3	18	5
15		2	1	5	5	4	15	4.5
16		4	3	5	5	4	17	4.5
17		4	4	5	5	4	18	4.5
18		5	4	5	5	4	18	4.5
19		4	1	5	5	3	14	4
20		5	5	5	5	5	20	5
21	A	4	2	4	4	1	11	3
	B	3	6	5	3	6	20	5.5
	C	1	7	2	6	3	18	4.5
	D	5	3	6	1	2	12	2.5
	E	2	5	7	2	7	21	6
	F	7	4	3	5	5	17	4.5
	G	6	8	1	7	8	24	7.5
	H	8	1	8	8	4	21	6
22		4	2	4	5	4	15	4
23		4	4	5	4	2	15	4
24		4	4	5	5	4	18	4.5
25		5	4	5	5	4	18	4.5
26		5	4	5	5	1	15	4.5
27		4	2	3	3	3	11	3